# INTROVERTS

The Life-changing Introvert's Guide to
Overcoming Social Anxiety, Radiating Confidence,
and Conquering Fear!

(Maximize the Advantages of Being an Introvert)

**Gavin White**

Published by Harry Barnes

## Gavin White

All Rights Reserved

*Introverts: The Life-changing Introvert's Guide to Overcoming Social Anxiety, Radiating Confidence, and Conquering Fear! (Maximize the Advantages of Being an Introvert)*

ISBN 978-1-7778032-1-6

suggested remedies, techniques, or information in this book.

Upon using the information contained in this book, you agree to hold harmless the Author from and against any damages, costs, and expenses, including any legal fees potentially resulting from the application of any of the information provided by this guide. This disclaimer applies to any damages or injury caused by the use and application, whether directly or indirectly, of any advice or information presented, whether for breach of contract, tort, negligence, personal injury, criminal intent, or under any other cause of action.

You agree to accept all risks of using the information presented inside this book. You need to consult a professional medical practitioner in order to ensure you are both able and healthy enough to participate in this program.

# Table of Contents

# Introduction

Introverts hold powerful potential within themselves, oftentimes without even realizing it. Many of them give up without really trying. They have an inner feeling that there must be a better life out there. But they can't find a better life because they never learned how to see things as they really are. They suppress their inner strength instead of embracing it.

You can blame genetics, self-esteem issues, or a lack of confidence, but sometimes it's not that straightforward.

We have been weighed down by misconceptions and false assumptions that have led us to believe that we have an incurable plague of some sort. That kind of thinking encourages us to accept the inevitable and just give up on our lifelong dreams.

Some of us give the fake it till you make it approach a try, only to realize that something is still missing. It's easy enough to keep up with the act, until we end up exhausting ourselves from having to constantly be on. The approach works, but not always as well as we would like.

Both genders have argued that their side has it easier than the other when it comes to embracing introversion. Gender arguments are nothing new, and they will persist in the subject of introversion, just as they will in almost any other topic.

Many males argue that we have to be extroverted if we want to get the girl. How can males take the initiative as a leader if we can barely speak in public? Many females argue that they must be flirtatious at all times if they wish to be interesting enough. They believe that males are expected to practice stoicism, and therefore, there is no pressure for a guy to find success in relationships or at work.

Both sides bring up some valid points, but at the end of the day, introverts (male or female) are in the same situation; maybe not exactly the same, but within the same vicinity. Both genders want to experience the benefits of introversion while downplaying the darker side. Everyone has goals that can get sidetracked by the darker side of introversion.

The darker side of introversion can give others the wrong impression. Others begin to wonder why we are the way we are. They assume the worst; that we're stuck up or boring. If you ever overheard someone at a party or in a classroom talking about how quiet you were, they probably didn't say, "Oh, that person's cool. Haven't you ever heard of an introvert?"

Most people don't understand or even care to understand introversion. They'll simply expect us to keep up with the pace or be left behind. They'll tell us to get over our shyness, as if shyness and introversion were the same thing. People don't care why we aren't social. They don't care about the reason for inaction, they only care about the inaction itself.

It can isolate us from good experiences if we're not careful.

But there is also a very good side to introversion; an awesome one in fact. It's no big secret that some of the greatest artists are introverts. We have unique gifts that are ready and waiting to be used. The dedicated introvert always finds a way. But we have to stop seeing ourselves as victims of introversion.

We might not need to grow out of being introverted, but we need to break away from the things that are holding us back in life.

So how do we stay true to ourselves without crushing our success in the process? What if we need to be extroverted? How do we emphasize our strengths? How can we enjoy life without exhausting ourselves? Why do introverts love their solitude, yet sometimes find themselves daydream about being more outgoing? Is introversion just an excuse for not having to deal with the pressures in the external world?

This book will address those concerns and answer those questions.

With that said, there are also different types of introverts. Although all introverts can benefit from this book, it is directed slightly more towards introverts with shy tendencies. These are the introverts who love their time alone, but also feel the need to go out and socialize more. If you'd like to make the best of your solitude, but at the same time, feel the urge or have the obligation to succeed in an extroverted arena, this book is for you. If you want to stay true to your introverted self while overcoming the obstacles that introverts face, this book is for you.

# Chapter 1: The Power Of Introverts

J.K. Rowling, Barack Obama, Audrey Hepburn, Warren Buffet, Bill Gates, Albert Einstein, Mark Zuckerberg – these are just some of the most popular names in history and in the modern world, and they all have something in common – their introverted personality. They are known as icons and leaders in their own chosen fields, and all of them admitted that they are introverts. The success of these icons proves that introverts have a place in this world that seems to favor people who have excellent social and interpersonal skills.

Introverts are often perceived as socially awkward and shy, but the truth is that they are full of extraordinary skills and talents that are waiting to be unleashed. In contrast to extroverts, who can be easily distinguished by their more readable dispositions and outgoing nature, introverts prefer to stay alone, keep things to themselves, and think carefully before they take action and interact with others.

Most of those who have introverted personality are also often wrongly perceived as people who don't like to be in the company of others, or who are not skilled enough when it comes to socializing. However, note that this is not true most of the time. Introverts love to be alone and value peace and quiet, but this does not mean that they don't have friends. In fact, their social circle, no matter how small, is composed of people whom they truly trust and whom they can give their unconditional love and loyalty to in return.

They don't typically need other people to inspire or motivate them. They can easily find sources of inspiration and motivation within themselves. Introverts are deep thinkers, and they have several qualities that make them ideal for powerful positions, success and leadership. They are passionate about the things that they love, which is one of the reasons why there are thousands of introverts who have succeeded in their chosen undertakings.

Signs That You Are An Introvert

If you feel like you are an introvert, but are not a hundred percent sure yet, then check to see if you display the following signs of introversion:

You dread attending an event with too many people

You love being alone

You prefer to observe, rather than talk

You have a rich inner world

You love to spend time by yourself

You find it awkward to initiate or take part in small talk

You love to talk about the topics that you are passionate about, but only to your closest friends or loved ones

You feel the need to take a break after spending some time with too many people

You prefer to have only a few friends who are truly close to you, instead of collecting too many acquaintances and casual friends

You love to spend time with only a small group of people

You tend to listen and observe more than you talk

You are passionate about solitary activities, such as reading

You have a space that you consider as your own; this is where you go when you feel like you have exhausted all of your energy after spending a lot of time in public

You don't share what you feel and think with others that easily

You love activities that allow you to use your creativity and imagination

If you have most, if not all, of the signs indicated above, then it means that you are an introvert. However, let it be clear that just because you are a natural introvert, this does not mean that you should worry about not having a place in this world; your natural personality does not need to be a limiting factor in what you can do. You actually have a very important role to play in society, and people will start to look up to you if you just know exactly how to tap into the power of your unique personality.

Embrace your introversion, as there are several reasons why being an introvert is beneficial not only for you, but also for the people around you. Here are just some of the many positive and powerful qualities shared by introverts:

Excellent Listening Skills

Introverts have excellent listening skills. In fact, they listen and observe before they open their mouth to speak. They observe from the sidelines, taking a few mental notes before making their presence known in a social situation. This gives them enough time to prepare, making them more confident when they participate in a conversation since they no longer have doubts pertaining to the accuracy of the words that they are saying.

Self-Sufficient

Introverts don't depend on others to survive. They are independent. They don't love the idea of depending on others to satisfy their material and emotional needs. This kind of freedom makes a lot of introverts empowered since they are fully aware that they are capable of managing any challenge that life will throw at them.

Focused

Most introverts can focus on things intently. They pay close attention to non-verbal cues that may expose hidden meanings. They are fully aware that the words people say are just half of the entire story. This skill helps them prevent misunderstandings, making it easier for others to deal with them.

Easy To Please

Another positive quality of introverts is that they are easy to please. They don't need a lot of material things to be content and happy. In fact, they prefer to stay at home and enjoy their time alone, instead of going to loud bars and buying costly drinks. Such a unique trait allows them to manage their finances effectively, relax (even after facing a stressful situation), and be happier.

Trustworthy

Do you have secrets that you want to share with someone who is sure not to reveal them? Then try sharing them with an introvert. Introverts are known for their ability to keep secrets. They know how difficult it is to trust someone, so you can expect them to keep your secret in confidence. This is the main reason why introverts perfectly fit the bill as excellent best friends. Their trustworthy nature also makes them capable of keeping long-term friendships.

Driven And Disciplined

Introverts are fully committed to their goals. Since they don't desperately seek the approval of others, they are capable of expending their energy on pursuing their goals. This is one of the reasons as to why there have been a vast amount of highly successful introverts in the past and present, and there are sure to be many more in the future!

Thought-Provoking

Introverts can display this trait once they find the courage to come out of their shell and talk. They are thought-provoking conversationalists in the sense that they have several interesting points to add to almost any discussion. It is true that introverts typically don't like small talk that much. However, this does not mean that they can never be engaging once they participate in deep discussions.

Introverts are typically more reserved, yes, but that does not mean that they don't love the company of other people at certain times. They just choose when they should talk and when they should get themselves involved in a discussion.

Since they are passionate people, you can't expect introverts to waste their energy and time on shallow and trivial conversations. To bring out the fascinating and thought-provoking traits of an introvert, you need to ask them smart questions about specific topics that they are passionate about.

Mysterious

"Mysterious" is one of the first words that people tend to use when describing an introvert. Introverts usually come across as mysterious because they don't talk that much. This means that those who are around them often find themselves having to guess what is on their mind.

Introverts are also masters of their own emotions. Most of them are capable of not displaying what they truly feel on their faces. Most of them don't brag, boast or show off, especially when they are in a social setting. They are in full control not only of their emotions, but also of their moods and body language.

While there are times when this trait may be disadvantageous (since it may cause other people to perceive them as aloof or snobby), there are still a lot of cases when they can use their mysterious personality to their advantage. It can even make those who are around them think that they are concealing several intriguing secrets, when what they are actually thinking about may be as simple as what they will be cooking for dinner.

Introverts come off as highly intellectual, allowing them to easily gain the respect of others. They can manage to attract other people despite their quiet nature. They are mysterious and this trait often makes them more magnetic, leaving those who are around them to wonder what they are actually capable of doing.

See? Introverts have a lot of amazing traits, so you don't need to be ashamed of your personality if you have just realized that you are one of them. Be proud and learn how to overcome your social anxiety, boost your confidence and conquer your fears in order to make the most out of your introverted personality and to be an inspiration to others.

# Chapter 2: A World Of Duality

Think about the traditional American executive. Do words like 'assertive', 'persuasive', and 'socially confident' come to mind? For me, it does. You see, society has placed a certain stereotype we have to fit into if we want to have success. It's in our collective ethos to strive to develop these extroverted qualities. Unfortunately, most people think that only through acquiring these traits can one be successful or happy. This why many introverts feel inadequate growing up; they are pushed to be something they're not.

I've experienced this many times in my childhood. Adults seemed to worry about my lack of social ability and constantly pushed me into making friends. Let me give you an example. During recess, everyone in class would go out to play. Personally, I preferred to stay indoors on my own. I never understood how my classmates could prefer to run around in the madness that was the school playground during recess hours. Even today, as a 'full-fledged adult', it's hard for me to be in loud places or around people with very loud voices (sorry if you're one of them). Ten-year-old Gerald was in bliss at his desk playing cards. The same couldn't be said about Gerald's teachers or counselors. They thought something was wrong with him. Next thing I knew, I was getting daily pep talks from family and teachers alike, encouraging me to be like the rest. It felt suffocating because I wasn't allowed to be me.

I think it unnecessary to describe how this pattern continued in high school, college, and the workplace. As an introvert, you're pushed into being something you're not throughout your entire life. It's almost cruel to think about. But that's how America and most of the western world works.

What About the Rest of the World?

Asians are known for their more reserved attitude. Take a country like Japan, for example. In Japan, being the loudest or trying to stand out too much is seen as unattractive and presumptuous. For instance, during speech, they tend to take the spotlight off themselves and prefer to place it on others, usually through compliments. The receiving side is expected to either downplay his/her work, or to 'out-compliment' the other side by something along the lines of, "Thank you, but we know my input wasn't nearly as valuable as yours." This is a common sign of humility. Let me illustrate a few more examples:

In the workplace, a person with more experience and knowledge will be respected much more than one who knows how to speak well or persuasively.

In relationships, it's uncustomary to be flirty or pushy. Rather, more emphasis is placed on forming a bond with the person you're courting. It has been shown in studies that Japanese women feel more attraction for humble and submissive qualities in men than western 'alpha male' qualities.

The cultural ethos is oriented towards building character and values; very similar to ancient stoic philosophers who preferred a life of sturdy discipline and inner growth than one of instant gratification. Qualities like persistence, honesty, humility, and solidarity are highly valued. This is a big contrast from qualities valued in the western world such as autonomy, getting things done fast, self-confidence, and charisma.

How did it end up like this?

To understand the present, we must understand the past. If we look back enough we can begin to make sense as to why both cultures (Eastern and Western) deviated so much from each other and why they have preferences for different behavior.

The West

Western school of thought comes from the Greeks and the Romans. Most of ancient western philosophy revolves rational, scientific and logical schools. These schools attempted to explain worldly events by looking outside of oneself. This is how modern science developed.

This is evidenced in the undertakings of the past two centuries. Most of the technological innovation prior to the digital era happened in the western world. Even the space race took place in the western world (the USA and the USSR).

We have inherited this way of thinking, and it has become the foundation of how our society judges our behavior and what is expected of us. Aristotle is quoted as saying, "Excellence is never an accident. It is always the result of high intention, sincere effort, and intelligent execution; it represents the wise choice among many alternatives- choice, not chance, determines your destiny." The quote implies an outward view of success. It is something we can choose, pursue and can attain if we work hard and make correct decisions. A quick look at the majority of self-help books in contemporary times will reflect a very similar philosophy of success.

The East

The Asians had a completely different cultural heritage than we did. They inherited the teachings of the Vedas, Buddha, and of Lao-Tse among others. In the east, men were not judged as much for their outer achievement as they were for their inner triumphs. The Buddha once said, "Though he should conquer a thousand men in battle a thousand times, yet he, indeed, who would conquer himself is the noblest victor." The focus was placed within.

Perhaps the greatest example of this is the Buddha's own life. Siddartha Gautama was a prince that had acquired everything but was still unrest. He began a journey in pursuit of a life without suffering. And thus began his journey, which also turned out to be an inner one. His greatest battle, in the end, was an inner one. After conquering the demon he found whilst in meditation, he awakened. The Buddha preached, "Peace comes from within. Do not seek it without."

Eastern cultures flourished with the idea that all their efforts should go into exploring within themselves. As such, there is no coincidence that thousands of years later, a contemplative and introvert character is preferred in their people.

Neither is Better than the Other

Great wisdom can be found in both philosophies and neither is better than the other. However, for both to co-exist there must be a balance. But is there balance in our current state in the western world?

Not at all.

If you're an introvert, and you happen to live in a western society, you have found yourself stranded in the wrong part of the world. You'll have a tougher time here.

And this is the primary reason why introverts may feel inadequate about their own nature. However, and a Buddhist monk would probably agree with me, this problem is more about being able to accept yourself rather moving away or changing who you are.

# Chapter 3: Improving Relational Skills By Understanding Personality Traits

Recognizing personality traits can be tough, even if it is a very popular area of study. The obvious does not seem to be that obvious at all. More examples of personalities may help us in recognizing personality traits. Let's look into the lives of a few famous celebrities and well-known leaders.

Oprah Winfrey, Bill Gates, Martha Stewart. What do these three people have in common? First, they are all very successful. Second, we know that their personalities led to the success of their careers in their respective fields.

According to some experts, characteristics that make people more likely to succeed are seeing, thinking, imagining, motivating, and collaborating. When there are difficulties such as social and economic crises, these people rise above the rest and become the leaders. In previous generations, the same kinds of people became powerful and influential, just as our history books tell us.

However, though these traits are ideal, misunderstanding how they work can result in unrealistic dreams and goals. Sure, you can succeed with these traits, but to truly become effective in what you do, you will need the ability to be strategic. Recognizing personality traits related to this is therefore imperative.

In recognizing personality traits, people respond and evaluate themselves based on behavior and temperament. Adjectives often used as answers include being outgoing, dependable, caring, and so many more. Sometimes the answers are professions - you're a doctor, a psychologist, an engineer. Rarely will people ever respond by enumerating their habits and tendencies.

Personality traits are those that are most natural to you-the qualities that you don't even realize that you have. Here's an example. During team meetings, your boss often asks for suggestions from everyone; or sometimes he randomly drops by to ask you a question. You and your colleagues are not surprised by these actions, because they're expected as part of his personality.

Some personality traits are quite predictable assuming that all the ingredients are present to insinuate a person to react according to his patterned behavior. For example, during your monthly meetings, you already knew that one of the managers would never dare to challenge the boss. In other words, it's not the nature of the person to go against the current, and it's almost impossible to see him acting this way.

When circumstances are familiar, recognizing personality traits also becomes easy. Certain situations bring about certain reactions that will always be the same given a similar circumstance.

Therefore, you develop a pattern and people will most likely know how you will react. If for example, in a heated discussion, you know that one particular individual will not defend his case or shoot down another person's ideas. It's natural for that person to never challenge others; so that same reaction is expected of him every time you're in a meeting.

Recognizing personality traits helps us interact with others better. It is especially helpful in the workplace, where there are many possible disagreements, misunderstandings, and lack of communication. By having a broad understanding of people's personalities, it will be easy to predict their tendencies in specific situations and adjust your actions accordingly. This will definitely improve your interpersonal and team dynamics skills.

Having dwelt extensively on the subject matter of personality and its traits; we will do well to narrow down our discourse to the notion of an INTROVERT simply for the essence and scope of this e Book.

# Chapter 4: What Do Introverts Want?

Being alone feels like a place to the introverts, as if it is a state of being or maybe a room where they could treat themselves for being who they really are without anyone trying to judge them or label them as shy, reserved or asocial. I like to commute in public transport; I like to sit alone on the window side and look outside. I like having my time with myself to gather my thoughts and reorganize them' It helps me refuel myself, it gives me a chance to reflect on what's to come and to inspire the inner being, just to be who I am and who I wish to become.

See, for me it's not ju st a bus or a train ride, there is a random music playing on somewhere, there is a movie going on in the background. I like the sound of birds chirping outside, the sound of a sky train approaching a station, just these random sounds and noises. Everything is in slow motion when you are an introvert, you don't just look at things/people, you observe them, it seems like the earth has come to a standstill. There is a story; everyone out there is a character; someone, who plays a particular role in their own story may be altogether play a different role in someone else's story, maybe I am a character in someone's story, I have no idea what role I play, good or bad or if I play any role or not. There is someone out there who is thinking about their dreams, working hard trying to realize and fulfill them, someone who is trying really hard to pass an exam, to clear an interview, someone who is running late for a meeting thinking about what their boss will say and how and what will they say in explanation, all these people are struggling with something or the other, which I have no idea about. This is really interesting, in my head at least.What I don't like in the public transport is rushed, sleepy, gloomy yet tired and angry faces, and the proximity to individuals in the crowded buses is something that I hate. Some people think commuting with introverts is, like a nightmare; it's not that they don't like people instead they don't want to miss the once in the lifetime opportunity to experience a new story that plays daily; that's why for introverts commuting with someone is just like missing this entertainment. The commute time is really important to an introvert, during the day. They like to engage in activities that don't require much socializing, they like the stuff like thinking deeply, sitting alone organizing their thoughts; bus rides, walking in a park, rowing a boat, visiting quiet places like library, museum and temples/churches. They like slowing down in this fast pace world either with someone or by themselves. There are people who like the journey more than they like the destination, who like solitude rather than companionship, yes, we exist, we are the introverts.

Introverts even like things that sound funny to others but is an important part of their daily activities for instance scribbling on a piece of paper; they try to draw all their imagination on this little piece, they really like scrolling through social media and the time when they hit the like icon on random pictures on social media instead of commenting. Another thing to notice among introverts is many of them prefer using emoticons over words while chatting. For introverts weekend is their time; they like going to all their favorite places so, whenever you need an introvert, they will be there with you, even if the occasion is little crazy, a little loud, they may have to use the bathroom to recharge themselves occasionally; but they will have fun. If I visit you, I would like you to understand that I would like to leave a little earlier than anyone else not because I hate it or I am bored but it is because I lose energy for being around people and being over-stimulating, but I will let you know when I am not feeling comfortable being around people.

Introverts are gullible, they usually are not able to see through the lines, if you are cheating on them they will trust you blindly, however if you break their trust they might not say much but inside their mind there will always be a fire burning, a fire of vengeance and revenge; there are chances that they may forgive you but they will never forget what you did with them.

The world needs to understand that talking and being around people is what non-introverts want, to feel energized and to feel alive. However, I want you to know that if you want to spend time with me, I would like too but I will need a break after a certain time to charge myself up. I want you to respect that I am reserved, I don't open up easily. I am the one who struggles, connecting with people, I am the one who wants to be included but fears getting drained with too much human interactions. Once we step into this, we need our time to revitalize ourselves like while in the gym, I like working out alone, I am one of the few people who like going to work it's not because I love working or something like that but because I know I will be by myself at my workstation and with my work, and there will be lesser human interaction than at home. I don't want to talk much to my family and friends either, that's why my attendance at school and colleges would be way more as compared to family get-togethers.

The l ighthouses don't go running all over an island looking for boats to save; they just stand there shining that's how introverts are; grace with energy and joy, guard very carefully; open up occasionally. World needs you and the things that you carry, try to find the best of all possible journeys and the courage to speak softly, welcome the world and let them welcome you the way you are, be the way you are, be an introvert and be it with pride.I don't believe anything really revolutionary has ever been invented by committee, I am going to give you some advice that might be hard to take. That advice is: If you are an introvert and you want to perform better then work alone, not on a committee, not on a team.

Your solitude will be a support and a home for you, even in the midst of very unfamiliar circumstances, and from it you will find all your paths. We need to understand a secret to life which is putting oneself in the right lighting, not all plants grow in the same conditions, they all need different type of soil, weather, water and nutrients to grow, similarly for some people it's a spotlight, a lamp lit desk for others it may be darkness that keeps them working and energized. Some people love to cancel out plans because they are too afraid to attend a function or be surrounded by people, they do this really frequent to such an extent some people consider this as their hobby. I believe blessed are those who do not fear solitude, who are not afraid of their own company, who are not always desperately looking for something to do, something to amuse themselves with, and something to judge, who don't want someone's company, someone to tell how amazing they are, or someone to talk to. I was just confused about why I was feeling overwhelmed all the time and trying to adjust to having people work for me.

I have been told enormous times to come out of my shell but some people fail to realize that some animals naturally carry shelter everywhere they go and some humans are just the same.I don't have time for superficial friends, I am my own friend, I like talking to myself when I am lonely; if we don't talk to ourselves at least once a day, we miss an opportunity to talk to an extraordinary person. I think our imagination functions in a much better way and efficiently when we don't have to speak to people or when there is no one around us. For introverts, to be alone with their thoughts is as restorative as sleeping or relaxing on a bean bag, always remember it is as nourishing as eating. We should always acknowledge people who are capable of doing things alone all by themselves, and there are people whom we need to be beware of, those who seek constant crowds; because in my view they are nothing when left alone.

Introverts are self-sufficient they spend a lot of time on their own and they shut off quite easily. For them loneliness is the state of not being able to enjoy solitude, introverts enjoy their solitude like no one else does. A happy life must be to a great extent a quiet life, for it is only in an atmosphere of quiet that true joy dares live. When I am alone, I can become invisible. I can hear the almost un-hearable sound of the flowers singing.

Most people draw energy from backslapping and shaking hands and all that, I draw energy from discussing ideas with myself. Wise men know, when to speak and when to stay quiet. Solitude has its own very strange beauty to it; we need someone to be able to see it. You do not need to leave your room, remain sitting at your table and listen, not even listen, simply wait, be quiet, still and solitary, the world will freely offer itself to you to be unmasked, it has no choice, it will roll in ecstasy at your feet all by itself, you just need to be quiet. As an introvert, you can be your own best friend or your worst enemy. The good news is we generally like our own company, a quality that extroverts often envy. We find comfort in solitude and know how to soothe ourselves. Our visions will become clear only when we can look into our own heart. I think I am a weird combination of deeply introverted and very daring. I can feel both those things working. I really like to stay in my nest and not move, my tiny little bubble where there is no one threatening to burst my bubble or step into my territory. I travel in my mind, and that's a rigorous state of journeying for me; however, mybody isn't that interested in moving from place to place. I would rather sit on a pumpkin and have it all to myself, than be crowded on a velvet cushion. Introverts, may have strong social skills and enjoy parties and business meetings, but after a while they wish they were home in their pajamas. They prefer to devote their social energies to close friends, colleagues, and family. Introverts are capable of acting like extroverts for the sake of work that they consider important, people they love, or anything they value highly. I want to be left alone because sometimes being in crowd makes you feel more alone than being by yourself. One thing that the world needs to understand is if an introvert opens up to you, that means you are very special for them but that happens rarely, very rarely.

Sometimes quiet people really do have a lot to say; they are just being careful about who they open up to. A bored person is someone who deprives you of solitude without providing you with company. People are always so boring when they band together. You have to be alone to develop all the peculiarities that makes a person interesting. If you think you know me, you might be mistaken, study me as much as you like, you will never know me completely. I differ a hundred ways from what you see me to be. People think, in order to be open to creativity, one must have the capacity for constructive use of solitude, one must overcome the fear of being alone; but it's not true. It's not about becoming a fake extrovert,it's really about acknowledging the valuable traits that an introvert brings.

# Chapter 5: Embracing Your Introvert Side - Knowing What Comes Naturally To You And What You Need To Work At

Of course, introverts are not perfect, and that's why there are some things that they need to work on so they could improve themselves. This is not so that they could become extroverts but so that they could live life in a better and more meaningful way. This means that while you are able to accept yourself for whom you are, and that you're grateful for what you have and what you are able to do, you're still willing to work on yourself so you could be better.

How can introverts improve themselves? Here are a few simple ways:

Just go on and talk. Sometimes, the problem lies in thinking too much. While it's good that introverts think before speaking, they should also learn how to control their thoughts so they would not over-think. If you're stuck somewhere with someone, just go on and talk. It would certainly break the ice and get the conversation going.

Let what you do speak for itself. Make sure that you are able to create pieces of work that would make others admire you, not because you would like to be admired as a person but because you would like them to realize that you can produce substantial results and that being introverted is not a hindrance. Produce excellent work and people will certainly ask you for help, and more so, they will look up to you, too.

Don't be scared to take credit for your work. There's nothing wrong about giving yourself credit when it's due. You worked hard on something so you deserve recognition for it. If you're working with a group and you feel like they're making you feel less than you are, remember that it's okay to stand your ground and remind them who did the work in the first place.

Sometimes, you just have to put people in their place so they'd realize that you're not one to be messed with.

Learn how to set uncomplicated, attainable goals. Of course, it's okay to dream big especially if you know that you can work hard for it. But sometimes, you have to realize that you have to set short-term goals so you would feel fulfilled once you have completed or achieved some of them. In turn, you would be all the more inspired to go forth with your long-term goals. Start small and see how great, big things could come from it.

Learn how to ask for help. Remember that it's definitely okay to let your guard down and ask for help—especially if you know that you can't do something on your own. You'll be more productive this way.

Know that it's okay to relax. You don't have to get your mind working all the time. Know that it's okay to chill out and give yourself time to breathe—without it, you won't be able to keep on working all the time and you won't be able to feel good about yourself. Relax and take it a day at a time.

# Chapter 6: Managing An Introverted Personality

Since there are different types of introversion, it's important to do some self-analyzing in order to find how to best succeed in the world. Just like having a natural flair for design or numbers, introverted individuals have a wealth of valuable qualities waiting to be utilized. This chapter will help to identify those qualities and aid individuals in becoming an introverted success in any field.

Recognize Your Strengths (Hidden Strengths of Introverts)

The benefits of being an introvert can be an asset in just about any social setting. However, perhaps what makes introverts so compelling to be around is there unique way of focusing. Since introverts take in so much information at once with their excellent skills of observation, they tend to be able to hone in and focus on just one thing with extreme detail. Rarely will one find an introvert spreading himself or herself too thin over a wide variety of projects and so what often results is a single project executed with quiet efficiency. Additionally, this singular type of focus makes for extremely skilled introverts; instead of being mediocre at 10 different things, they'll be phenomenal at 3-5 of them, given the time to master each skill individually. This is a huge asset for the work place as well as personally, when free time can be spent mastering pursuits that the individual loves.

All of that focus requires an immense amount of internal processing as opposed to the extrovert's way of verbally bouncing ideas off of other people. Because of this silent version of processing, introverts are able to maintain a persona of calm even when they feel anything but. Don't mistaken, introverts can experience the highs of emotion just like extroverts, but more often they are able to outwardly control their temper and keep their cool, a super strength when it comes to the workplace or raising children. Rather than immediately trying to solve a problem, introverts will think it through first and then act when they've discovered the most direct and reasonable solution. For the workplace, this skill is most useful in high stress and pressure occupations, like law or the stock market. As for families, anyone with children knows that patience is key, and introverts have it, or at least can appear to have it, in spades.

Just as an introvert's focus gives way to a cool exterior, that calm demeanor translates to excellent communication skills. Because they tend to think before they speak, introvert's spoken thoughts are often direct, decisive, and well thought out. This is equally powerful in writing, a favored profession for many introverts. Communicating effectively and clearly in the smaller circle of acquaintances that most introverts prefer also allows them to create deeper and more meaningful relationships than someone who is spreading their time between large groups of people. The workplace benefit of this is that clients are apt to feel more cared for by an introvert who listens and appropriately responds to their needs. Socially, this skill makes for some dinner parties and one-on-one conversations where the introvert is fully engaged in the conversations and those lucky enough to count an introvert as their friend feel that they are being heard. Of course, this also makes for wonderful family dynamics, in which each family member is receives a special spotlight of attention or valued alone time with his or her introverted family member.

Overcome Fears and Anxiety

Fear and anxiety are emotions that plague all introverts, albeit in different ways depending on their type. Here are some particular fears that an introvert may be experiencing depending upon their type of introversion as determined by Cheek's study.

**Social:** Individuals who are social introverts may experience anxiety over public meetings, though not in ways typically expected. An introvert may not fear being in large groups at all, but rather find it exhausting and view it as an ordeal, which then causes the anxiety, particularly if excuses have to be made to a friend who is reluctant to hear them. The best way to deal with this is for the individual to either politely decline the invitation and explain to the friend that they find small talk stressful or practice this particular kind of communication beforehand in order to be able to navigate large social gatherings more easily.

**Restrained:** Because restrained introverts take the time to think deeply before they speak, it can be difficult to get a word in while talking in groups. It may cause anxiety for some or even the fear that an introverted individual may never have the chance to say what's on their mind. In this case, it's important to be assertive. Of course, don't interrupt others in order to get words out, as that is probably what causes some introverts to remain silent, but when a gap opens in the conversation, introverts should stake their claim and finish their sentence strongly, as opposed to trailing off. While this can be difficult, practice will make it easier.

**Anxious:** Anxiety can arise very easily for a restrained introvert, who tends to meditate on past, present, or potential future occurrences. Where the anxiety comes in is when the individual continually thinks about unpleasant until they are left with a feeling of extreme ill will, even after they have distracted themselves and engaged their mind in a project or other topic. One way to deal with this type of introversion is to practice meditation in order to take the mind of off stressful topics and instead concentrate on positive and productive ones. In regards to the anxious introvert feeling awkward when forming new relationships, try to practice these skills like a social introvert and stow away open ended questions that can be used to find out about the other person and create a relationship without having to do too much talking.

**Thinking:** Of all the different types of introverts, the thinking introvert should have the least amount of anxiety in public settings. Where anxiety can arise, however, is getting lost in the conversation because what is happening in the individual's mind is actually much richer and fulfilling. This can create a problem if the introvert is in a workplace setting, for example, and lose track of the conversation because their mind is already ten steps ahead. While this is a valuable resource and quality, it is not ideal for meetings with people such as clients or students. Additionally, it can make matters awkward when caught in a lost moment in the middle of a party if someone asks the introvert a question and they introvert has been somewhere else mentally. In these cases, it's important to stay focused and in the moment, doing one's best to save introspective reflections for alone time.

Develop Communication Skills

It's already been established that introverts have impeccable conversational skills when in small groups. However, what step can one take when faced with a need to step away from the conversation and recharge, or when confronted by a large group of people? Below are three tips to help battle overstimulation and disinterest, and heighten listening.

Choose Your Own Establishment: This means setting the stage for your meetings, whether they are professional or personal. Choose a spot that is small and quiet, preferably with calm colors and little to no music. This will help introverts to keep from becoming overly stimulated and allow them to remain active in the meeting longer. Choosing this location will also aid listening skills since there will be no need to strain in order to hear the other person. And speaking of listening…

Ensure Optimum Listening with a Time Limit: Many introverts, particularly social and restrained ones, express a deep need to step back and recharge after being in a prolonged social situation. This recharging moment is crucial if an introvert is going to absorb and process a great deal of information. So to ensure great listening, insert breaks throughout the conversation in order to step back and take a few deep breaths alone. Using the bathroom is probably the easiest excuse, however introverts should take their environment into account before the meeting and evaluate valid reasons for stepping back and places to do so. If this makes some uncomfortable, it is perfectly courteous to politely say excuse me and just walk away. If the meeting is with a family member or friend, consider letting them know ahead of time that time to recharge is a necessity.

Keep The Meeting Short: If it's within the introvert's power, the meeting should be kept short to whatever time the introvert is comfortable with. Additionally, the time limit should be verbalized ahead of time, making for a smooth and graceful exit that everyone is prepared for. This allows introverts to place their full concentration on the meeting and alleviates the fear that the meeting could go on indefinitely. This time limit also sets a deadline for introverts to voice their opinions that may have normally been saved for a later time. Most importantly, however, is the time limit will keep introverts who desperately need to recharge from switching to an automatic mode that will severe hinder listening and potentially hurt relationships.

# Chapter 7: Dealing With A Lack Of Confidence (Or Shyness) In Social Situations

**A** common misconception is that introverts are shy people. This isn't always true (but yes, some shy people can be introverts as well). In fact, a lot of introverts can be very sociable and breathe life into any party. Just because someone is an introvert doesn't mean they're antisocial, nor are they necessarily shy. But in the end, being around large groups of people for extended periods of time will typically tire out an introvert. Sometimes, though, it's just plain necessary to go out with friends or colleagues in order maintain relationships, build your professional reputation, or expand your network, even though it can be hard to motivate yourself when the couch is calling your name. Consider these questions and answer them honestly:

☐ Is shyness and insecurity a problem for you?

☐ Are you afraid of looking stupid in social situations?

☐ Do you worry a lot about what others think of you?

☐ Do you frequently avoid social situations or cancel at the last minute?

☐ Do other people seem to have a lot more fun than you do in social situations?

☐ Do you assume it's your fault when someone rejects you or seems uninterested?

☐ Is it hard for you to approach people or join in their conversations?

☐ After spending time with others, do you tend to dwell on and criticize your "performance"?

☐ Do you often feel bad about yourself after socializing?

If you answered "yes" to these questions, then you've always struggled with shyness or a long-standing difficulty making friends, you may believe that there's nothing to be done. But you don't have to live with shyness, or social awkwardness. None of us are born with social skills. They're something we learn—and the good news is that it's never too late. You can learn how to be more confident and secure in your interactions with others. You don't have to change your personality. It's simply a matter of learning new skills and adopting a different outlook. So recharge and regroup as often as you need and, when you're ready, get out there armed with these tips.

Tune In Before you go out

It can be helpful for introverts to take some time to regroup before heading into a big event, party, or household full of people (even if it's loved ones). Try sitting quietly in your car for 10 to 15 minutes in the driveway before going inside. Or if you commute on public transportation, take advantage of calming music or a meditation app to create the peace of mind necessary for introverts to recalibrate. You can also watch a feel-good movie, play some upbeat songs, or meditate/allot time for yourself. Make sure that you do something fun or relaxing before a social gathering so you don't feel stressed out and get the urge to drink. Wear comfortable clothes and inhale. And don't forget, if you don't want to be in any given place at any given moment, no one is forcing you to go. Always choose your battles wisely!

Take a break.

Need a little room to breathe? Excusing yourself to get a drink or use the bathroom (even if you don't actually have to) can be great opportunities to find pockets of solace at overly crowded events. You can sneak out for a walk when you're locked into even lengthier situations like weddings, holiday parties, or conferences. And don't worry—people are so wrapped up in their own conversations that you can slip in and out without raising eyebrows.

Know when to say no.

Of course, there comes a point where you need to turn down some invites. You need to make room in your schedule for some serious downtime. Although no two introverts are exactly alike when it comes to a set number of commitments that tip them over the edge, take note of which weeks feel more overwhelming, and use those to determine an upper limit on how many obligations you can handle. It's equally important to tune in to our bodily cues. You know at a cellular level when you're losing steam—you may start to feel restless, bored, and even headachy. If you're itching to get out of a situation, it's OK to leave a little early or decline an invite to hit yet another bar. Say something like, "I've had a blast, but I'm going to head home now. Let's pick this up another time.'" Being an introvert is nothing to worry about. Yes, exiting your comfort zone when it's necessary for your career or maintaining social ties is important. But tuning in to your innate sense of when enough is enough takes priority.

Fake it 'til you make it.

People will respond more positively to you when you project confidence. What's more, simply acting as if you're confident can make you feel more confident. Focus externally, not internally. People who lack social confidence tend to be in their heads when interacting with others, thinking about how they're coming across or worrying about what they're going to say. Try to switch your focus from yourself to the other person. You'll be more in the moment, plus you'll feel less self-conscious.

 Tackling social fears

When it comes to shyness and social awkwardness, the things we tell ourselves make a huge difference. Here are some common thinking patterns that undermine confidence and fuel social insecurity:

☐ Believing that you're boring, unlikeable, or weird.

☐ Believing that other people are evaluating and judging you in social situations.

☐ Blieving that you'll be rejected and criticized if you make a social mistake.

☐ Believing that being rejected or socially embarrassed would be awful and devastating.

☐ Believing that what others think about you defines who you are.

If you believe these things, of course social situations are terrifying! But the truth isn't quite so black-and-white.

People aren't thinking about you—at least not to the degree that you think. Most people are caught up in their own lives and concerns. Just like you're thinking about yourself and your own social concerns, other people are thinking about themselves. They're not spending their free time judging you. So stop wasting time worrying about what others think of you.

People are much more tolerant than you think. So what about the embarrassment in the moment when you say or do the wrong thing? In your mind, the very idea is horrifying. You're sure that everyone will whisper about it and judge you. But in reality, it's very unlikely that people are going to make a big deal over a social faux pas. Most people will just ignore it and move on. When you realize that social mistakes don't have to be devastating, it's a lot easier to put yourself out there.

When you start realizing that people are NOT scrutinizing and judging your every word and deed, you'll automatically feel less nervous socially. But that still leaves the way you feel about yourself. All too often, we're our own worst critics. We're hard on ourselves in a way we'd never be to strangers—let alone the people we care about. Changing your self-image for the better isn't something you can do overnight. Learning to accept yourself requires changing your thinking. You don't have to be perfect to be liked. In fact, our imperfections and quirks can be endearing. Even our weaknesses can bring us closer to others. When someone is honest and open about their vulnerabilities, it's a bonding experience. If you can accept your awkwardness or imperfections, you'll likely find that others will, too. They may even like you better for it!

Some social fears are fairly minor, and you can get used to them pretty quickly. But for more intense social fears, you'll need a more detailed—and gradual—plan of attack. When it comes to the things that really scare us, you don't want to just jump right in before you're ready. That's like diving into the deep end before you've learned to dog paddle. What you want to do is face your fears in a gradual yet systematic way, starting with situations that are slightly stressful and building up to more anxiety-provoking situations. Think of it as a stepladder, with each rung a little more stressful than the last. Don't move on to the next step until you've had a positive experience with the step before. Once you get past your shyness and adopt a more self-accepting mindset, you may find that you do just fine in social situations. But if you still have trouble making conversation and navigating socially, you'll need to work on your social skills. Improving social skills requires practice. Just as you wouldn't expect to become good on the guitar without some effort, don't expect to become comfortable socially without putting in the time. There's no shortcut. That said, you can start small. Take baby steps towards being more social, then build on those successes.

☐    Smile at someone you pass on the street.

☐    Compliment someone you encounter during your day.

☐    Ask someone a casual question (at a restaurant, for example: "Have you been here before? How's the _____?")

☐    Start a conversation with a friendly cashier, receptionist, waiter, hostess, or salesperson.

Go to a party and ask a simple question (e.g. "Do you know what time it is?"). Once they've answered, politely thank them and then excuse yourself. They key is to make the interaction short and sweet. Ask a friend to introduce you to someone at the party and help facilitate a short conversation. Pick someone at the party who seems friendly and approachable. Introduce yourself. Identify a non-intimidating group of people at the party and approach them. You don't need to make a big entrance. Just join the group and listen to the conversation. Make a comment or two if you'd like, but don't put too much pressure on yourself. Small friendly interactions such as these can be very positive and confidence building. And if certain interactions end up feeling a little awkward, there's not a lot at stake.

Tips for making conversation

Some people seem to instinctively know how to start a conversation with anyone, in any place, be it a party, bar, health club, the checkout line, a crowded elevator, or on public transport. If you're not one of these lucky types, don't despair. Here are some easy ways to engage in conversation with someone new

Remark on the surroundings or occasion. If you're at a party, for example, you could comment on the venue, the catering, or the music in a positive way. "I love this song," "The food's great. Have you tried the chicken?" or "That's a great view." Ask an open-ended question, one that requires more than just a yes or no answer. Adhere to the journalist's credo and ask a question that begins with one of the 5 W's (or 1 H): who, where, when, what, why, or how. For example, "Who do you know here?" "Where do you normally go on a Friday?" "When did you move here?" "What keeps you busy?" "Why did you decide to become a vegetarian?" "How is the wine?" Most people enjoy talking about themselves so asking a question is a good way to get a conversation started.

Use a compliment. For example, "I really like your purse, can I ask where you got it?" or "You look like you've done this before, can you tell where I have to sign in?" Note anything you have in common and ask a follow up question. "I play golf as well, what's your favorite local course?" "My daughter went to that school, too, how does your son like it?"

Keep the conversations going with small talk (This will be discussed in the next chapter). Don't say something that's obviously provocative and avoid heavy subjects such as politics or religion. Stick to light subjects like the weather, surroundings, and anything you have in common such as school, movies, or sports teams.

Listen effectively. Listening is not the same as waiting for your turn to talk. You can't concentrate on what someone's saying if you're forming what you're going to say next. One of the keys to effective communication in any situation is to focus fully on the speaker and show interest in what's being said. Nod occasionally, smile at the person, and make sure your posture is open and inviting. Encourage the speaker to continue with small verbal cues like "yes" or "uh huh."

Note - Stuck in a deathly boring conversation, there are some "stop" signals that are still socially appropriate. Try being very still, as if you are waiting for the other to finish, then looking down or away can communicate to the other person that you're ready to move on. You can also try interjecting during a pause in the other person's monologue: "Great meeting you, but I've got to go say hello to the host/refill my drink/visit the restroom

Dealing with social setbacks and rejection

As you put yourself out there socially, there will be times when you feel judged or rejected. Maybe you reached out to someone, but they didn't seem interested in having a conversation or starting a friendship. There's no question: rejection feels bad. But the important thing to remember is that it's part of life. Not everyone you approach will be receptive to starting a conversation, let alone becoming friends. Just like dating, meeting new people inevitably comes with some element of rejection.

The following tips will help you have an easier time with social setbacks:

Try not to take things too personally. It's hard not to take rejection personally, but social interactions don't happen in a vacuum. The other person may be having a bad day, distracted by other problems, or just not in a talkative mood. Always remember that rejection has just as much to do with the other person as it does you.

Keep things in perspective. No one likes being rejected, but it doesn't have to devastate you. Remember that someone else's opinion doesn't define you, and it doesn't mean that no one else will be interested in being your friend. Learn from the experience and try again.

Don't dwell on mistakes. Even if you said something you regret, for example, it's unlikely that the other person will remember it after a short time. Stay positive; refrain from labeling yourself a failure, or from telling yourself that you'll never be able to make friends

These simple tips will make going out a whole lot easier. And just remember: Going outside your comfort zone into situations that can benefit your career—or doing something for someone you love—will work in your favor in the long run.

# Chapter 8: How To Become An Extrovert

Although it is not easy to become a more extroverted person, it is not impossible. Here are some of the most effective techniques that you can use to make your transition a bit easier.

What kind of extrovert do you want to be? When you want to become more extroverted, you need to imagine yourself as the kind of person you want to become in the future. If you have a negative view about extroverts then you will have a hard time becoming one yourself. You do not have to become the kind of extrovert that you hate (the shallow, noisy ones that annoy you to no end), just someone who is more sociable. Imagine yourself as someone who is comfortable hanging out in a room full of people and actually speaking to some of them. If you can imagine yourself in that kind of situation then you are already one step closer to your goal.

Think about what you have to offer to other people, instead of the other way around

Most introverts think that there is no point in socialising if they cannot get anything out of it. Stop thinking like this, and instead think about what other people can get from interacting with you. Think about the kinds of things that you are knowledgeable about, it does not matter what they are. You can be an expert in the lore surrounding the Lord of the Rings, your extensive knowledge about anything automotive, or your uncanny movie trivia knowledge, you can share your peculiar knowledge with other people, and they will somewhat find it interesting. If you share what you know, it will not take long before other people will share their own particular brand of knowledge with you. Remember, relationships are always give and take, so think about what you can give to other people first and not the other way around.

Socialise with your kind of people

There is no point in trying to fit in a group where you are uncomfortable, hang out with the kind of people whom you like. For instance, if you are already thirty-something, it will be easier for you to socialise with people within your own age group or with people who are a bit older. At your age, trying to fit in a group composed mostly of college students or fresh graduates will only make you feel awkward.

Join a club

As mentioned earlier, one of the ways to increase your extroversion is to hang out with people with whom you share a common interest/s, and there is no better way to find those kinds of people than joining a hobby club. Are you interested in gardening? Join one of the many garden clubs in your town. Are you a book fiend just like most other introverts? Join a book club and attend the weekly meetings where the members discuss the books on their reading list. You do not have to join all the clubs that pique your interests, in fact, if you find that you are uncomfortable in the club you joined, just quit and look for another one. All you need to do is find that one good club, that one that engages you intellectually and you actually like hanging out with the other members, and you will get your recommended amount of socialisation for an entire year.

Work on your social skills

The previous chapter discussed about lack of social skills being one of the main reasons why introverts prefer to stay the way they are; they always think that they will only embarrass themselves in front of other people so they will do anything to avoid interacting with others as much as they possibly can. Fortunately, you can work on your social skills; and you will learn more on this in the following chapter.

Keep in mind that you are not only depriving yourself of the benefits of socialisation, you are also depriving other people from knowing the real you. Who knows? That special someone who you are meant to spend the rest of your days with may be in the crowd of unfamiliar faces, while you on the other hand is still moping at home.

# Chapter 9: Building Confidence When Communicating

Lack of confidence is one of the reasons why introverts choose not to participate in social interactions. You can build your confidence by doing the following:

Practice your communication skills

The best way to build self-confidence is to view all your social interactions as a form of training to develop your skills. The more interactions you get, the better you become at talking to people.

Your past successes in communicating however, should remain in the past. If you stop interacting with people for a prolonged period, your skills will begin to deteriorate. The only way to keep your communicating skills at a high level is to keep practicing.

Keep learning about communication

Just like when practicing any other skill, you need to observe your performance to be able to make adjustments. You should look into the areas of communication where you need to improve.

You should then observe how successful people use the same skills and emulate them. Over time, you will have a collection of best practices in communication.

Give yourself opportunities to use your skills

If you will only be spending your time with a few people, you will not develop your communication skills. You should look for more opportunities to practice your skills by participating in more events.

You should make a list of events that you got invitations for and then try your best to attend every one of them. You may also look for social events in your area where you can meet strangers. If you are religious for instance, you can go to your local religious activities.

You could also increase your interaction with new people by joining volunteer work. In these activities, you will not be forced to make unnecessary interactions.

You can build new relationships and be productive at the same time.

Widen your social circles

You will become more confident if you see progress in your social skills. As mentioned earlier, most introverts only speak with familiar people. You can try to improve your own social skills by expanding the size of your social circle. In essence you're making yourself familiar with more people.

To do this, you should make a list of the people you talk to regularly. You could list the people you live with, the ones you communicate with at work and other social groups you may be a part of. Most introverts only constantly communicate with less than 30 people. When talking with the people in your list, try to learn more things about them that you did not know before. Use your questioning skills to learn more about them.

You can expand your circles by meeting your friends' friends. For instance, if some of your friends like attending concerts, you could come with them and start interacting with the new people you meet. If you interact with 30 friends on the regular, you have 30 opportunities to meet new people. If you keep doing this activity, you can significantly expand your network within the year.

Accomplish goals consistently

You can also improve your confidence if you keep accomplishing your communication goals. In the beginning, you can create simple goals like talking to one coworker per day. As you become better in communicating, you can set goals that are more ambitious. For instance, you can set a goal of closing deals in your work or meeting new business contacts in a local business club.

You can build your confidence for completing important goals if you consistently complete the most important ones first.

# Chapter 10: Be A Powerful Introvert Leader

Many scientific studies have shown that introverts make powerful, persuasive and effective leaders. Just because they prefer to be alone and silent most of the time doesn't mean they can't influence their teams and businesses and lead them to greatness. They have deep expertise, careful attention to details, intense focus, and excellent listening skills, among others.

You can be a remarkable leader. You do not have to be limited by society's presumptions on your personality. You are perceptive, intense and profound. Use these strengths to your advantage to guide, manage and influence the people under your leadership to be more productive and successful.

Here are 10 potent tips that can help you overshadow your perceived placidness and be a powerful leader in a predominantly extroverted world:

Focus on your strengths.

As an introvert, you have the following strengths. Learn to build on them.

- You think before you talk.

In both professional and casual settings, introverts carefully ponder on what is happening and what is being said before they respond. As an introvert leader, you will find that you often sit back and listen to everyone's ideas and with your silence, you encourage other people to express themselves. It is a good setting for more creative ideas to bubble up. You give people the chance to be heard. You measure each concept carefully to avoid mistakes.

Think about it: the quietest person in the room can be most powerful. Your calm demeanor will be heard above the corporate noise.

\-        You don't think too much of breadth as you would depth.

Introverts prefer a deep dive over many broad ideas. One of the strengths of an introvert leader is focusing on consequential, profitable conversations. They will not move on to a new idea unless they have delved into subject matters that are of importance. The introvert leader will ask meaningful, in-depth questions and take time to hear out answers. They will pursue understanding of what is happening within the organization and bring engagement to a deeper level.

You will find the introvert leader going around, asking questions from employees and seeking to see areas of improvement. They are able to discover and retain top talents to bring more effectivity to the organization.

-       You    are    low-key,    calm    and
composed.

Introverts can handle organizational crisis
well. They exude a confidence that can be
quite    reassuring.    Introverts    speak
unhurriedly    and    softly    despite
circumstances  or  heated  conversations.
They  are  always  prepared  because  they
plan in advance and rehearse before they
face   other   people   or   stand   up   in   a
meeting.

The  introvert  uses  preparation  time  to
psyche  themselves  up  and  feel  more
confident and positive. They know how to
silence negative thoughts and focus on the
task at hand.

-       They  can  articulate  well  with  their
hands instead of their mouths.

Introverts  have  a  special  love  for  the
written   word.   They   find   comfort   in
communicating     something     through
documents    instead    of    face-to-face
interactions. This is a good thing because it

helps introverts express themselves clearly, to get ideas and feedback, and to coach. They know how to leverage social media tools to craft new opportunities to connect with their team, their employees, and their clients.

-        Introvert leaders are not afraid of solitude.

As the old adage goes, "it can be lonely at the top". Introverts do not have a problem with that. Quite the contrary, they get energized by being alone. After they "suffer" from exhaustion by being around people, they embrace timeouts to fuel their creativity, boost their decision-making and enhance their thinking processes.

Being alone will cause introverts to be more responsive and manage interruptions. When they are recharged, they will be able to best manage what is expected of them and lead people to success. They become more consistent and clear with their commitments and these qualities will cause his team to trust him more.

Lead by example.

Words can be empty and actions always speak louder. When your employees or team members see how you work and how you lead, your skills and your passion, you can inspire them more than any charismatic speech would.

Know that "powerful" is subjective.

A lion doesn't have to say it is a lion, it just is. The same is true with powerful people. Many introverts are powerful and they don't have to be in other people's faces. So just be yourself, believe in yourself and you will do great.

Lead when needed.

You don't have to micromanage and talk all the time. The key is to find your A-players and let them do their jobs. You need only to say something when you need to lead them. Intelligent, efficient team players need vision and direction, not micromanagement. When you speak less and lead only when necessary, your words will be held in value and with respect.

Learn effective body language.
Did you know that you can trick your own body into believing you are very confident? Face a mirror and stand in a "power pose" for about five minutes. You will feel a change in your demeanor. Stand and act as if you are powerful and you will discover that you are opening yourself up to different situations with strength and confidence. Allow your mind to believe, and you will soon find yourself being so.
Find a strong partner.
Find someone that will bring balance, a mentor or a business partner who will help you lead discussions, approach strangers. Steve Jobs was a loud extrovert while Steve Wozniak was a timid introvert.

Together they worked well and established a strong company.

Go for smaller meetings.

Instead of having big networking events, have smaller meetings such as a lunch when you want to touch base with your colleagues, co-workers or clients. Not only will you have undivided attention and more quality time, you will also shine in comfortable social situations.

Always remind yourself of your unique power.

Introverts are pretty special – they rarely speak but when they do, something profound goes out of their mouths and inspires people. People will be surprised to know that introverts can also be funny. As an introvert leader, use this special attribute to draw people to you when you have something relevant to say at the most opportune time. You will find that the people around you will listen to you better and your words will carry more weight.

Don't be afraid to articulate your ideas.

Commanding influence is one of the key qualities of a leader. Do not be afraid to present your ideas even in large groups. If social situations such as big conferences or board meetings intimidate you, it will not hurt you to find dynamic ways in which you can communicate your thoughts comfortably. Some ideas include email, blog posts, small talks, or brainstorming with a few key people.

Don't focus on your weakness.

It is important that you apply your optimal skills in leadership. Do not put emphasis on what you are not or what you don't have. It is counter-productive. You are a unique individual with unique strengths and skills. For instance, as an introvert you can instinctively listen to your team and identify areas you need to make necessary changes. You are very good at problem solving. Use these traits to make a difference instead of thinking how different you are.

You don't have to focus on being powerful to be a powerful leader. Just be effective. Do not concern yourself over small things such as being shadowed by an extroverted colleague. Be you and be effective then you can successfully influence and lead others.

# Chapter 11: Does It Matter Where We Meet?

Does it matter where you meet for the first time if you are dating an extrovert? Does it matter how you meet? Where should you go on your fist date?

Where to Find Romantic Contacts

Although I met my husband through friends and that is a great way for introverts to meet potential dates, there are many others as well.

The Internet Match Game

It is much harder as an introvert to get started in the dating game, but once we do, we have many advantages over extroverts. In getting started, one of the most difficult aspects is how to meet the right person when you hate socializing and you hate small talk. For introverts, the answer just might be the internet. Though I never tried this myself, I certainly have introverted friends who have and who have done so with success.

When it comes to dating, the internet can be a two edged sword. For many people, there are hidden dangers in seeking dates or mates online. There are all kinds of security issues and issues of authenticity. However when it comes to the introvert, dating and matchmaking sites just might look like the Promised Land. Why? With online dating services, the introvert is able to search through a wide variety of profiles of potential dates and select a few she/he is interested in.

This saves the introvert from all the bars, parties and socializing to find a date. Perhaps the best thing about the internet for introverts is the chance they have to talk with potential dates as often and as long as desired and needed to feel comfortable. Then when you do feel comfortable with someone, you can meet for lunch in a public place and go from there.

Two introverts meeting online and going through this process might be well on their way to a committed relationship by the time they have that first public date. On the other hand, if you are choosing to converse with an extrovert there might be a few mores steps and dates you have to take before you get to the long term relationship.

When using the internet in this way, the introvert needs to be very aware of the security on the sites they are using. Make sure that security is built into the site and safety is their priority. If the site is legitimate and secure, then the internet can be a gold mine of potential life partners for introverts.

Keeping everything said here in mind, the internet is a terrific tool for the introvert in terms of dating. Introverts love the internet and we love email. These are tools we can control. We can set our own pace in conversations and decide who can and who cannot access our thoughts and ideas. Handling at least the early portions of the dating relationship through online tools also gives us as introverts the time we need to process each step along the way, and to be ready before we take the next step.

Introverts Meeting

Two introverts might do well to meet one another on the internet. Matching services, chat rooms, dating services all give introverts the opportunity to meet and talk as long as they want or need to before meeting face to face. There are some things you need to do before interacting with anyone on an online match or date service. Here are a few tips for the introvert who wants to use an online site to meet their potential dates.

Spend some time browsing the site extensively before you begin an interaction with anyone. Find out about the security on the site and the moderators. How does the site work? Do you have to pay to use it?

Check out how many ads are on the site. If it is a free site it will have ads to pay for the site. However if the page seems to be nothing but ads – avoid it.

If you are willing to pay a fee, try the reputable sites like eHarmony, Match.com and Christian Mingle. That way you at least know you can trust the site.

Now register and be honest about yourself when answering the questions. If you truly want to meet someone compatible with you, then you have to be honest about whom you are.

Do not give out personal information like address, phone number etc. at the early stages. Wait until you are sure you will be safe in doing so.

Before you make any arrangements to meet in person with anyone, go to the site's chat room and meet there first. Chat online until you feel it is safe to meet in person. When you meet in person for the first time, meet for lunch at a very public space and when lunch is over say goodbye and perhaps make another date. But do not go beyond lunch on the first date.

You might ask others on the site if they know the person you are meeting and what they think of them.

Locales

For the introvert, there will be a very different set of locales where they might meet a romantic interest than the one the extrovert will have. Extroverts are going to congregate in places where there are a lot of people, places where 'small talk' leads to dates and relationships. I know from my experience that I hate these types of places and do not engage well in small talk. Most introverts will feel the same way.

For the extrovert, the place to meet a potential partner includes bars, parties, business conventions or get togethers, and clubs of all kind. These are places the introverts are likely to avoid if it is at all possible. Introverts will be found through online dating sites, private small parties, church groups or hobby groups. You might meet at work, by chance or through a few of your friends. Introverts can meet potential dates in any of these places just as the extrovert can. The real question is what is the best place to meet potential dates? You can try all the traditional ways but when it comes right down to it, we introverts are better off being innovative and going outside the box to meet potential soul mates.

Other places where you might find others include:

Volunteer for something you truly care about. Do not just volunteer to meet someone. Make sure you genuinely care about what you are doing, and then you will have the chance to meet others who have the same passion. This is also true of clubs or organizations. Just do not risk you authenticity and integrity to find a partner or the relationship will not last.

There are these days Meetup Groups for Introverts. These groups will put you in touch with a large number and a wide variety of introverts. The only problem with this is I can anticipate it getting a little depressing if you do not quickly find someone there.

Taking a class in something you are genuinely interested in is also helpful as you will meet people with like interests both introverts and extroverts.

Another good place for introverts to meet potential dates is of course the workplace, however there are many cautionary tales regarding this. If you are going to date someone from work make sure it is an equal. Do not date a superior or if you supervise people do not date a subordinate. The only time it is acceptable is when you are both on the same level.

Where to Go on Your Dates

Now that you have met someone you want to date and perhaps build a long term relationship with, the next question is where do you go on the first date that you will be comfortable. If your date is with an introvert, this issue is of course a lot easier. However let's suppose you are going on a first date with an extrovert. He will want to go to dinner or a party. He might want to go to a sporting event or a philanthropic event. The key word here being event – and as an introvert you really do not want to have your first date with him to be at an 'event'.

Remember I met my husband through friends then we went to a movie, and after that we went to dinner.

So what are the best places to go on a date?

Coffee shop

Movie

Small gathering of friends (no more than 6).

Perhaps a physical activity if you enjoy them such as bike riding or trail hiking, bird watching or horseback riding - just the two of you.

Museums are great ideas for introvert first dates. There are art museums, history museums, children's museums, specialty and science museums. If there are aquariums or planetariums in your area, those are great places to start.

You could also go to the zoo or botanical gardens.

If you know that both you and your date enjoy rides, you could go to an amusement park.

A concert or philharmonic might keep things calm and on an even keel, while giving you the space to get to know each other.

As an introvert, you will not want to go anywhere that makes you uncomfortable or unable to process what is going on with your date because the atmosphere around you is too hectic, crowded and noisy. If you cannot relax and spend quality time with your date because you are at a party of over 50 people, or you are at a sporting event, then you will be frustrated and uncomfortable through then entire date. That is exactly what you want to avoid.

# Chapter 12: Finding Your Way In Life As An Introvert

Or, how to find your introvert sweet spot

Even though there is a growing awareness of introverts and our particular set of gifts and positive attributes, we still live in society where extrovert values rule. We are told to build our personal brand, grab the spotlight, take the lead, make our voice heard.

In the business world, open floor office plans and lively group meetings and brainstorming sessions are the way work gets done.

In school, quiet kids get called on when their hand isn't raised and are expected to work frequently in large groups.

In social settings, the "life of the party" are those social butterflies that can make small talk with anyone and mix and mingle as if their life depended on it.

Where does that leave the rest of us – the quiet ones who work well on our own, who can end up feeling overwhelmed and depleted in a room full of strangers?

In my life, I spent many years regretting my introvert tendencies. Regret without reflection is wasted energy. Turn any regrets you might have into deep reflection and steady action.

Reflect On Your Gifts

"Gifts" might sound like a heavy word to you. But it's simply one way to describe the unique amalgam of attributes, skills and natural inclinations that make up your personality. Remember, the word "gift" means that you don't need to keep them to yourself – share your unique skills and attributes with other people to really make them shine.

So, let's make a list. What are you good at? What do you have to offer at work? In a relationship? With friends and family?

Here's my short list:

- I'm deeply loyal
- I love to listen and help people
- I anticipate other people's feelings

- I am considerate of other people

- I am a hard worker

- I can focus deeply on problems and troubleshoot solutions

What's on your list? Write it down. Keep your list somewhere you can easily access it. Read it often. Memorize it. This will help shift the way you see yourself in relation to the world.

You Are More Than an Introvert

This book is all about making the right moves to thrive as an introvert in the world. But it's important to remember that, although introversion is an important part of your personality makeup, it's not the only part of what makes you unique. Are you a soccer player? An artist? An entrepreneur? A stand-up comedian? A sensitive person? An intellectual? These are all part of your personal mosaic.

Personally, I take great comfort in identifying myself as an introvert. I remember being a child in school and feeling strangely out of tune with many of my classmates. While everyone else seemed to love competitive sports, working in groups and the noise of the playground, I longed to be with a small group of friends, or enjoying some quiet time in the library. I wish that someone had said to me, "It's okay. You're an introvert. Your inclinations and feelings are totally normal." What a relief that would have been!

But . . . if calling yourself an introvert makes you feel limited or "locked in" in any sense, it's time to shift focus away from the label. Remember that introversion exists on a long continuum. Remind yourself that it's not an "either/or" scenario. You don't have to choose between acting like an extrovert or an introvert. You simply have to exist and remind yourself that there is ample space to move around the spectrum. Some days you may feel more extroverted than others. That's normal and healthy. You are not limited to living in a box. You are more than one word or one thing.

Life Hacks for Introverts

Now, I want to share some highly actionable tips designed to help you move through the world with confidence and make everything a little more fun. Here we go.

Learn the Art of Making Small Talk

Extroverts have a knack for striking up conversations everywhere they go. Even if you hate small talk, sometimes there's no getting around it. And here's a little secret for you: making small talk is actually not that hard. Here are some pointers:

- Keep it light. Stick to topics that are upbeat. Small talk should be fun, so you should probably avoid grim subjects like crime, the struggling economy, war, etc.

- Steer the conversation toward a topic you find interesting. Part of what makes small talk so challenging for many introverts is that it can seem so frivolous. Small talk suddenly becomes much more engaging if you can talk about something you are curious or knowledgeable about.

- Seek out extroverts. My first instinct at any large social gathering is to seek out fellow introverts. However, if you find yourself stranded at a cocktail party without anyone to talk with, make small talk with the extroverts around you. Extroverts are naturally good talkers; introverts make naturally good listeners. See where I'm going with this? It's a complementary fit. The danger here is getting trapped in a one-sided conversation. You can counteract this by asking questions and being ready to excuse yourself if you find yourself feeling trapped.

- Encourage stories. When you are talking to someone you don't know very well, it's a great opportunity to learn and gain fresh perspectives. Ask open-ended questions that encourage the speaker to provide long answers, and possibly even stories. An easy way to get to know someone is to ask, "What do you do for a living?" But be sure to follow that up with: "How did you get into that line of work?" Getting people to tell their stories is the best way to connect at a deeper level.

- Remember this golden rule: arrive late, leave early. If you have any control over when you can arrive and leave any kind of large social or professional event, use it. Make it a point to arrive a little late – not late enough to offend your hosts or cause disruption, of course. Simply arrive late enough so that the event has already gotten underway. The idea here is to minimize the amount of time and energy that you have to spend socializing, without missing out on meeting new people and enjoying the event. If you arrive early at an event, chances are you'll start feeling drained and ready to go home halfway through the night. Take care not to drain your social battery too fast.

Make a List of "Personal Rechargers"

I'm going to ask you to make one more list. It's a doozy. My question for you is: how do you rest? How do you recharge? What makes you feel new again?

Personally, I feel recharged after I:

- Get a good night's sleep
- Walk my two dogs
- Read a good book
- Have a long chat on the phone with my mom (or another good friend)
- Enjoy a glass of wine with my husband
- Take a bubble bath
- Go for a walk on a nice day

If you notice, five of the things on my list are things I do on my own. Because I am an introvert, I enjoy spending ample times of alone because it's when I do my best, deep thinking. It's how I unwind and relax. Now, it's not the only way I relax and recharge. But this time is central to my mental, physical and spiritual health.

So, now it's your turn. What makes you feel new again? Make a list and keep it close to your heart. When you're feeling overwhelmed, go back to the list.

# Chapter 13: Be Aware Of Your Mental State

Some introverts prefer to stay away from the crowd because there are certain factors in there that they do not like. In your case, you need to identify them and exercise the strategies in this chapter to deal with them in a socially healthy way.

Identify the factors that make you irritable

Some people become irritable when they are in a crowd. There are certain factors that may cause their mood to change. For some, it is the noise, while for others; it is the heat that is emitted from the group of people.

Introverts like to take in and internalize information before reacting to it. When in a crowd, an introvert automatically takes in information and experiences. He then takes the time away from the crowd to internalize the information he has gathered.

There are times, however, when people can become overstimulated. This happens when there is an overwhelming amount of information. For most adults, there are certain factors that cause frequent overstimulation of the senses. Some, for example, become overstimulated of the sight of too many people. Some also become overstimulated of the experience of many people talking at once. Introverts tend to become sensitive to these slight sources of irritation because they do not prefer spending time with a lot of people. If you experience becoming irritable with a crowd, you need to identify the factor that causes you to become like that.

Strategies to prevent overstimulation

For most people, their awareness of the specific things that make them irritable in a crowd is already enough to help them control their behavior so that they can calm any anxieties or crankiness. If this is not the case for you, there are two things that you can do to prevent the effects of overstimulation of the sense.

Avoidance

The first strategy is to avoid the factors that you hate. For example, if you hate loud noises, you can move away from the crowd as they begin to become loud. Although avoidance is an easy option, it may not be the best for your personal growth. By avoiding the problem, you are allowing it to dictate your actions and ultimately determine the limit of your confidence.

Limit exposure

One effective strategy is to expose your mind to the factor that irritates you but in limited intensities. In the case of loud noises, you can stay with the crowd even though people are starting to become loud. You should only stop when you can no longer control your mood. As you gain more experience with groups of people, you will begin to become accustomed to the factors that affect your mood. By gradually exposing yourself to the factors that affect your state and mood, you can learn to overcome them with time by slowly becoming desensitized to the negative effects.

Train your mind to block out distractions

You should also train your mind to avoid focusing on these distracting factors. In environments where there are a lot of sensory inputs, you should limit your focus on the things that matter for the task at hand. By focusing your mind on the important thing, you will limit the input that your brain receives and prevent information overload.

In busy, loud and crowded environments, the eyes are the sense organs that will guide your brain on what to focus on. If you need to listen to a person speak, but there are many distractions in the environment, you should make your eyes focus on his lips. When you do this, you can see how his lips move as he speaks. Instead of taking in all the information around you, you can focus on the speech of that person.

Control your mood when you are feeling irritable

There will come a point when you will begin to feel irritable over the environment ruled by extraverts. The loud noises and the constantly high number of people in one place may become stressful for introverts.

When you feel signs of irritability, you should identify it as soon as possible. By identifying the problem you have already taken an important step to overcoming it. You should then use deep breathing (which will be described in the next chapter) to keep your mind under control. By keeping your mind calm, you will be able to last longer in the presence of big crowds.

# Chapter 14: Recharge Your Batteries

It is no doubt that too much socialization is tiring for the introvert. Remember, we find fulfillment in looking on the inner world.

I like to think that introverts have a social battery. After recharging it fully, they go out with a lot of energy. But as they start having conversations and meeting new people, this battery gets drained. Of course, it is not all conversations that drain it. Some actually recharge it.

When this imaginary battery becomes too low, the introvert has no choice but run back into his shell to recharge. Otherwise, being in a state of low battery for too long means every new conversation becomes irritable. In fact, he may become annoying to even those around.

Once the introvert has recharged, he can then get back into the world to start socializing again.

A study showed that extroverts are stimulated by seeing people. On the other hand, introverts find satisfaction in looking at inanimate objects. These could be flowers, the sun, or anything around them. That's how they recharge their batteries. Here are other ways they recharge:

Reading a book

Watching a movie

Meditating

Journaling

Learning a new form of art

Napping

Gardening, etc.

How Much Alone Time is Too Much

However, while you must recharge your batteries every day, you do not want to be overdoing it. It is possible to spend too much time alone. And that is never a good thing. You must remember that humans are social animals. And we need to feel a connection with other people.

There is no universal agreed amount of time that you must spend alone. That cannot happen. Here are some of the reasons why:

First, remember that the level of introversion is not the same for all people. Although you may be an introvert, there could still be a considerable percentage of extroversion in you. So this means while you will need alone time, you will not need it more than someone who is more introverted than you.

Secondly, we have to also consider the activities you do to recharge your batteries. While someone will need just one book, someone may need 5. While someone may need to just watch one movie, someone may find meditation appropriate.

The last problem has to do with how fast you recharge. This also varies from person to person. You need to know how long it takes in your case. Of course, if you use too much of your social battery without recouping it, it will take longer to refill it.

It is difficult to realize that you are starting to feel lonely. That's because loneliness is not an object. You cannot walk into your mind and search for the reasons you are feeling sad. However, if you are in touch with your feelings, you may notice the tell-tale signs of loneliness. But you must take these with a grain of salt. Other reasons may be responsible for your sadness.

Here are some signs that you are starting to feel lonely:

Too much shopping – usually, we buy things because we want to fulfill needs in our lives. We buy clothes to protect ourselves from heat and cold. We buy shoes to protect our feet from dangerous objects.

Most of us already have the basics to live comfortable lives. If you find yourself buying too many things that you already have, or upgrading things, or buying things you may want, then you have a need in your life that needs fulfilling. And you believe possessions may do the trick.

Unfortunately, possessions only provide fulfillment for short periods of time. So it won't take long before you start shopping again, hoping the next thing you purchase will work.

Mostly, it is lonely people that indulge in behaviors like these. This was proved in a study of 2500 people who were followed for a period of 6 years.

You start getting bored with the things you love – if you enjoy reading books, you may find yourself not enjoying them. You may find you lack the motivation to focus on them.

This is another sign that you are missing something in your life. And that could be face-to-face interactions with others. You can be sure of this if you haven't been going out a lot lately.

You feel like spending more time with others – this is probably the best way to know that you are lonely. When you stay away from others for too long, every interaction seems so liberating. You may find that even though you don't hang out more, you are feeling that you should get out more. It's like your hunger of socializing gets dialed from 3 to 7.

You shows signs of stress – there are lots of causes of stress. And one of them is your life being devoid of happiness. And sometimes, happiness can come from being with other people. When stressed, you may have trouble sleeping, you may overeat, and you may become moody. You may also have trouble remembering things and difficulty in concentrating.

These things can lower your immune system, reduce your productivity, and speed the aging process. You also have a high chance of gaining weight and suffering from heart disease and stroke.

Knowing When You Need Some Me Time

It is just as important to know when you need some time alone. You may get carried away with socializing and forget that your nature requires you to retreat into your shell. Again, it is not easy to know that you need a break. You just need to interpret your emotions and figure out what they are telling you.

Your body screams for some Me time – whenever you are chatting with people, if you find yourself always searching for a way out, then your batteries may need recharging. This feeling will get worse the more you chat with people.

You are getting irritated easily – there are lots of things that may irritate you, from babies crying to spoons falling on the floor. If you get annoyed with little things like these, it means something is wrong. Your brain is probably stressed, which can be a result of too much socializing.

You have difficulty concentrating – this may happen when in social situations or even when at work. The thing is you are starving your mind by denying it something it desperately wants. And it will try to force some Me time, be it in front of others or at work.

Keeping the Balance

You don't want to be playing catch-up all the time. You need to live your life so socializing and recharging both have enough time. It is not easy to say how one can achieve this balance. For some people, they will need more Me time while others will need less. It all comes down to understanding what makes you tick.

How do you know how much time you need in your case?

Observation.

The trick is to use the tips above to know when you are getting more (or less) of one thing and make the necessary amends. If you are socializing too much, then cut back. If you are being alone for too long, then get out a little more.

To help enforce the balance, you must allot your time. Although this trick may not work in all cases, it gives you a basis to use. And you can increase time for socializing or recharging as needed.

For example, you can say that for 1 hour every day, I will be chatting. It may be with a friend, a colleague, or even a stranger. You can then say, for 2 hours, I will be recharging my batteries. If you want, you may even list the activities you will use to do that.

Of course, this plan is not to be followed in stone. Or you will find it too limiting and you will trash it. In addition, remember that every day is different. And so is every situation. In some cases, you will need more Me time or socializing than you normally do.

## Chapter 15: What Are The Key Strengths Of An Introvert?

Qualities that may be perceived as weakness are often an introvert's greatest asset. Think of introverts as an iceberg, what you see on the surface is only a small percentage of themselves. Here are some of the key strengths of the introvert.

● Active Listening

What is active listening? It is a skill that is incredibly valuable in most situations. Listening without hijacking a conversation and remaining engaged with the speaker comes naturally to introverts. Most people are busy working out what they will say next and are therefore less engaged with the speaker.

This skill makes introverts successful in certain work environments such as sales. You would normally expect gregarious people to excel in a sales place, but introverts can bring their own abilities and win over customers. Imagine a salesperson that actively listens to your needs, processes the information and responds accordingly perfect right?

- Excellent Written Communication

Verbal communication is definitely the field of excellence for extroverts, but they rarely have the same skills when it comes to the written word.

Writing comes naturally to introverts as it means they can take their time over the words they use and consider the best way to express themselves. Any break from the verbal thrusts that a lively conversation entails is welcome. Writing can also provide a haven of solitude for an introvert and allow them to recharge their mental batteries while still being productive.

A lifetime of writing will also help hone some pretty sharp writing skills and coupled with their skill for reflection generally produces great writing.

- **Independence**

Many people fail to recognize this personality trait in introverts and label them as unsociable. The truth is that introverts' value interpersonal connections just as much as other people, but they also need "me time."

Introverts also generate their own energy and do not need interaction with others to thrive. In the workplace, this translates as an employee that can be given a task and set free to complete it. This means there is no need for micromanagement and leaves your boss to concentrate on other things.

Socially an introvert has more successful relationships as they allow their partner's space to grow. If you are in a relationship with an introvert, you will never feel stifled!

- **Loyalty**

If you are friends with an introvert, you are honored. Introverts do not take friendship lightly. They will have considered you, your qualities and the part you can play in their lives. Because of this selection process, you can be assured of their loyalty at all times.

Connections for an introvert run deep. They do not take things lightly, and they will get to know you much better than your other friends.

Bearing in mind these qualities you should know that an introvert likes you because of your inner qualities and not just your public persona.

- **Consideration**

Introverts will not make snap decisions or act on impulse. It is not in their nature to have a snappy come back or a witty verbal retort on hand. What they do have is a mind that will contemplate all aspects of an issue before arriving at a conclusion.

The lack of impulsive behavior is a quality that makes introverts natural managers and executives in the working world. Solving problems without creating stressful situations help your workforce trust your decisions and respect your decisions.

Socially this consideration ensures that an introvert will never cause offense with an impulsive outburst or thoughtless action.

● Keep Calm and carry on!

The last thing you need in a stressful situation is someone who will ignite the mood and cause even more stress. An introvert will automatically keep calm and remain cool and collected no matter what happens. Sometimes it needs someone with a measured tone of voice to calm troubled waters.

Introverts have an inner "mind home" that keeps them centered no matter what storm rages around them. They will also be fully prepared before entering any situation and possess the mental tools that allow them to remain calm.

Introverts also have a rich imagination and will have considered every possibility that any situation can throw at them. This helps them keep a level head as very little surprises them or catches them out.

● Attention to detail

Introverts notice everything and have an unerring ability to pick up life's small details. This can be a trial as they see every aspect of tragedies and painful situations and take them on board.

This depth of insight can also be a huge asset. An introvert will know immediately when they are being betrayed or when someone is being false. They are deeply aware of every situation and if an introvert tells you that something isn't right then you must listen to them.

First and foremost, this depth of attention will help introverts on their quest to make the world a better place.

Finally, here are a few things introverts don't do that can be classed as strengths.

● They don't get bored working long hours

Introverts have an impressive ability to focus for long periods of time. They can thrive in positions that require longer hours than most positions.

● They do not miss appointments

If an introvert is late for a meeting, then their world is in turmoil. You can rely on them to meet deadlines and be punctual as long as nobody hovers over them.

● They don't hate people

Hate is a waste of emotion for introverts and they simply cut people out of their lives if they fail to meet expectations. This means that if you work with or are in a relationship with an introvert you will not have to deal with poisonous remarks about other people.

# Chapter 16: Make Time To Be Alone

Introverts with families and other personal commitments may find themselves feeling guilty if they ask for alone time. They ask themselves, if I'm spending all day at work or meeting other professional responsibilities, shouldn't I spend the little free time I have with my family or other loved ones? There are also introverts with packed schedules who fear that if they take some alone time, they would fall behind on their deadlines.

But packed schedules and family commitments should not keep you from taking some time off for yourself. Even finding an hour a day for alone time can do wonders in helping you maintain your personal equilibrium. The secret is to create practical and doable strategies that allow you to consistently eke out this time for yourself.

Here are some of our recommended strategies. You can try one or more of them or even mix and match them to better meet your particular needs. What is important is that you start to make small lifestyle changes over time and then decide what is most effective for you.

One simple technique is to wake up a little bit earlier. Many introverts find that waking up even just thirty minutes earlier did not necessarily leave them feeling more tired, since they were able to use this time for activities such as meditation or prayer, planning for the day ahead, or even just sitting quietly for a while and thinking.

What about staying up just a little bit later? You can also try it if it seems more suitable for your particular body clock, but many time coaches recommend waking up earlier since staying up can result in sleep deprivation.

Alternately, you can leave for work earlier and then spend some alone time in a coffee shop before you head for the office. You can plan for the day, read, reflect or just decompress. Or if you commute, you can shut off the phone and simply spend time alone thinking, reading, or doing other solitary activities.

You can also arrange to have a regular recharge time with your partner or loved ones. For instance, you can ask your partner to watch the kids for thirty minutes while you take your alone time. If you're a single parent, you can take some time to yourself after the children have gone to bed.

One activity that is particularly helpful for introverts is taking solitary walks. If you live near enough to your office, you can walk there instead of taking public transport or using the car. Or you can take some time to walk or even run during your lunch break. You can also use your gym workouts as your alone time. Instead of working out with a partner, you can do solitary workouts so that you can enjoy your needed mental space.

Another way that you can create mental space is by using an iPod or other device to play music, podcasts or other audio content when you want to be alone. You can play your favorite content during breaks while wearing earphones so that people would know that you are listening to something and don't want to be disturbed.

You can also make sure that you put coffee breaks and other breaks at work to good use. Instead of looking through your phone messages or visiting your Facebook page, use the break to get your alone time. You can perform activities such as writing a journal, reading a few pages of a book or magazine, or taking a short stroll outside.

# Chapter 17: Communicating Better As An Introvert

Our coexistence with other humans is mainly possible because we communicate. We communicate to pass on and receive information. But it goes way deeper than that. We communicate to feel loved and show love, we also communicate because we feel inclined to, that is only natural. The urge for humans to want to communicate is innate. In this chapter, there will be no theoretical analysis of what communication is or isn't. The focus here will be on how introverts can communicate better.

Anyone can learn to communicate better, including introverts. Yes, introverts do abhor small talk and would rather keep to themselves, but just like every other personality, introverts crave connections and good conversation. Below are some practical suggestions on how an introvert can communicate better and even initiate conversations.

Learn to communicate correctly

Pick the Right Time

Timing is very important when it comes to initiating a conversation. Imagine you've just been kicked out of your car by robbers and as you stare in bewilderment at the thieves speeding off in your car, a salesperson approaches, trying to sell you something. Would you be receptive to what the person has to say? Doubtful!

It's the same thing with conversations. You can't just dive into a conversation about the inner workings of your mind with someone who simply wants to make small talk. You have to be on the lookout for cues showing that the person is open to communication. Luckily for introverts, they're blessed with an eye that picks up cues that others wouldn't see right away.

Pick the Right Place

Communication for introverts also heavily relies on the environment. Picking a less stimulating environment is the best choice if you want to avoid draining your 'introvert battery.' For example, if you want to communicate in the workplace, it is best to avoid noisy places such as the lunch room.

Make An Effort

To truly master anything, you must make a consistent effort. Communication is no different. Listening already comes easily to introverts but what you can do to get more out of any conversation you listen to is ask questions. Instead of mulling over questions in your head, wait for a pause in the conversation and then chime in with your question. Because of the demeanour of introverts, it is easy for the person who is talking to feel like the introvert listening to them has zoned out or is not paying attention; by asking questions you prove that you were listening.

Face to Face

Many introverts prefer to text a person rather than call them. Text messages are great for casual conversations but when it comes to serious conversations, it is better to communicate face to face. This way, you can pick up nonverbal cues that you might not notice when you're having an electronic conversation. These cues can give you insights on whether or not your message is being communicated. While communicating, maintain eye contact, listen to what the other person says, and only interrupt if essential. While introverts tend to listen more, many people make the mistake of thinking that listening should be passive. You should listen with the aim of understanding the other person. If you don't understand, ensure you ask questions to clarify what is being said. You can also assist the listener to be an active listener by encouraging them to ask you questions if they need clarification.

Be Open to Learning

Learning communication is a continuous process. You'll come to find out that there's no one size fits all style for communication. For example, while some people prefer to have a conversation that slowly eases into the main issue, others prefer to grab the bull by the horns. Here are a few tips to help you communicate.

Ask open-ended questions to get people to talk more.

Avoid looking at your electronic device when someone else is talking.

Be honest. If you feel you're not being heard, say so. If you feel the person is not paying attention, calmly let them know how you feel.

Don't rush to fill in conversational pauses with more information. People sometimes need silence to process things.

Don't jump to conclusions. Let people say what is on their mind before you draw a conclusion.

Maintain an open posture. Avoid crossing your arms as it may send a message that you are not listening or that you disagree with what is being said. Also, avoid slouching.

Maintain eye contact but look away from time to time. Steadily staring into someone's eyes can be very awkward.

# Chapter 18: Communication Fundamentals

"Introverts are naturally adept when it comes to actively listening. We tend to be the friend or colleague you can call on when you're upset, or you have good news to share. We're going to be able to listen and be with you in that, without turning it around and making it about us."

Beth Buelow

We all know communication is important. Why else would you have bought this book? In this chapter, we will look at communication fundamentals—the core aspects of effective communications.

Let's begin by breaking down the elements of communication.

Slicing Up the Communications Pie

Here's some food for thought to start.

Consider the following and try to fill in the percentages:

What percentage of a message is conveyed by:

The words spoken: ___%

Tone of voice: ___%

Body language: ___%

Jot down your best guesses and keep them in mind as we progress. We'll reveal the answer shortly.

Let's start our discussion on the communication fundamentals by 'listening in' on a few business leaders in their day-to-day worlds, speaking to their employees.

The Leaders Share Strategy

What do you imagine about what each speaker feels about the message they are conveying?

Gerry is speaking about the new direction for the company. His voice is upbeat. His body stance is relaxed as he speaks to the audience.

Geraldine is making a presentation about the company's new business strategy. Her voice is strained. She is seated with her arms crossed as she is speaking to the audience.

Gerhard is sharing the company's new mission statement. He is speaking clearly but sternly. His back is to the audience as he is reading the slides.

Gloria is unveiling the company's new product line. She is speaking cheerfully and clearly. She stands and holds each new product up in front of her as she discusses its features.

Grace is announcing the company's new overtime policy. Her voice is even but a bit quiet. Her head is down as she is reading the details aloud.

With the small amount of information provided, what do you imagine each speaker feels about the message they are conveying? Would you feel more confident in your response if you could hear the speaker's voice? What if you were actually in the room?

10/40/50

Here is the breakdown of roughly what percentage of a message is conveyed by the words, tone of voice, and body language.

Messages are conveyed by:

The words spoken: 10%

Tone of voice: 40%

Body language: 50%

More specifically:

About 10 % of a message is conveyed by the words spoken. While spoken words are extremely important, their meaning can be distorted if the other elements communicate a contrary message.

About 40% of a message is conveyed by tone of voice. A voice tone that is loud, quiet, stern, cheerful, low, high, fast or slow will affect what the listener hears from the speaker.

About 50% of a message is conveyed by body language. Body language that conveys openness (uncrossed arms, eye contact, smiling) will cause a listener to take in a different message than the same words spoken with closed body language (arms crossed, no eye contact, frown).

You may have seen studies with slightly different percentages, perhaps from famous studies in the 1960s, but the principles are essentially the same: words matter, but tone of voice and body language can distort the message if they are not aligned.

Are you surprised at all by these numbers? Think for a moment about a time when you walked into a room in which someone later communicated a negative message. Did you pick up on anything in the person's body language that told you that something was wrong?

Think about a time when your boss had to give you negative news, either you were being laid off, or there was a performance concern. Were there cues in your boss's body language, in how he or she was standing or sitting? What about their facial expression? When they began to speak, was it clear to you that this wasn't going to be good news? What told you that, even if they were just greeting you? More than likely, their tone of voice foretold a bit of what was to come.

The words, of course, told the full story, but in these situations rarely is the fact that it's not good news a surprise by the time the speaker gets down to the message itself.

The 10/40/50 percentages carry these lessons when communicating a message to others:

Words are important, but they count less than you might think IF you send a different message non-verbally.

Body language is very powerful and can dominate a message.

If body language carries a message contrary to the words you use, then the intent of your message may not be believed or may not even be heard.

Tone of voice is worth paying attention to.

It is important to be congruent, as in your words, tone of voice and body language need to send the same message.

On the other hand, the 10/40/50 percentages offer clues when interpreting messages from others:

If you are discomforted by a message, try to notice what signals you are picking up on: the words, the tone of voice or the speaker's body language.

Be aware that the speaker may not even be aware that they are sending conflicting messages.

Remember that you may respond instinctively to voice tone and body language, and not even be aware of it.

If you notice that the message is not congruent, you have an opportunity to ask questions or otherwise determine what the real message is.

In most cases, you do not need to act in the moment, but should reflect on what you believe the whole message to have been.

We will delve more into non-verbal communication skills in the next chapter.

In this chapter, we will focus on listening and questioning skills.

Listening Skills

The best conversationalists put as much effort into how they listen as to what they say.

The best conversationalists:

Listen actively to the speaker.

Make eye contact.

Use non-verbal communication to signal understanding (nodding).

Ask open questions.

Respectfully allow the other person to finish.

Active Listening

As introduced earlier, as an introvert, you are naturally a good listener. When you apply yourself to learning active listening skills, you will be well positioned to take your natural abilities to a higher level.

Active listening refers to consciously paying attention to the speaker.

With active listening:

You give the speaker your full attention.

You concentrate on the speaker's words.

You pay attention to non-verbal cues.

You make a point of not allowing yourself to be distracted.

You do NOT think about your response.

You do NOT guess what the person means.

You do NOT interrupt.

You do NOT offer contrary information

If the person says something you believe is incorrect, or you do not understand, you WAIT until they have finished speaking.

Afterward, before responding, you ensure that you understand all of what the person has said. To do this:

You ask clarifying questions.

You summarize to confirm understanding.

If you feel you would like to take notes, at the beginning of the conversation you can say, "I hope you don't mind if I take a few notes. I don't want to forget anything you are saying." Then just take brief notes, as needed.

The benefits of active listening are:

There are fewer misunderstandings.

The speaker feels heard.

You are more likely to be listened to afterward.

Conflict is avoided.

The opposite of Active Listening is lazy listening, in which you pay little attention to what the other person is saying, think about what you will say in response, interrupt, don't pay attention to non-verbal communication or otherwise ignore the larger context. Lazy listening is ineffective! Ask yourself: Are you a Lazy Listener?

Your Last Vacation - Exercise

Ask a person to tell you about their last vacation. Use active listening skills as they respond.

As you listen:

Don't allow yourself to interrupt.

Ask questions only when the other person has stopped speaking.

STAY CURIOUS – keep asking more questions until you really have the whole story.

Don't interrupt to share your experiences.

Keep going until you have learned 5 things about the person and/or their vacation.

How did you do? Did you find yourself thinking ahead or wanting to interrupt?

Questioning

Have a look at these questions. What do you notice?

"Is this your first time here?"

"Do you like raisins?"

"Have you eaten rice cakes before?"

"What is that outside the window?"

"What type of cake do you prefer?"

"What's your favorite type of pasta?"

Need a hint?

What do you notice about the first three questions as opposed to the last three questions?

The first three questions are what are referred to as "closed questions".

The last three questions are what are referred to as "open questions".

What differentiates them is the type of answer they will solicit.

The Difference Between Open and Closed Questions

Closed questions invite one-word responses, which tends to 'close' down discussion.

Open questions, on the other hand, invite the listener to respond freely, which will naturally 'open' up discussion. Open questions open the door to dialog.

To enhance your conversation skills, you need to ask more open questions than closed questions.

EXERCISE:

Identify which of the following questions are closed vs. open questions:

"Do you like Italian food?"

"What are your boys doing for the summer?"

"Are your children boys or girls, or some of each?"

"Have you been to one of these networking events before?"

"What do you like best about this type of networking event?"

"Do you have anything to add to the discussion?"

"What do you have to add to the discussion?"

"Did you like this morning's speaker?"

"What did you think of this morning's speaker?"

Are Closed Questions Bad?

Closed questions are those that can be answered with "Yes", "No" or a single word answer, such as "Boys", "Three", "Tomorrow".

Are closed questions bad?

No, not necessarily, but they have their place.

Closed questions can be handy for getting quick answers to simple questions or for collecting information quickly. For example:

"Can you hear me at the back?"

"Can you see over me?"

"Do you want coffee or tea?"

"What day is your dental appointment?"

"Will you be in tomorrow?"

What other situations can you think of where closed questions might be most appropriate?

Create your own list but remember, to become an effective conversationalist, you need to master open questions.

Open Questions

An open question is any question that elicits an answer of longer than a single word.

The reason that open questions are preferred over closed questions is that open questions engage the other person and begin a dialogue.

EXERCISE:

You are at a conference and are waiting in line to get a coffee after a morning of speakers. What are three open questions you could ask your fellow delegates?

1.

2.

3.

**Tip:** You will probably quickly see how easy it is to fall into the trap of asking a closed question rather than an open one.

As open questions really can be your SECRET WEAPON though, it's worth spending time mastering this skill.

Open questions are a BIG ADVANTAGE that introverts can have over extroverts when meeting people.

Why?

Most introverts:

Prefer one-on-one conversations over speaking with groups.

Would rather have a nice long chat with one person than make a lot of small talk with many people.

Like interesting people.

As a result, mastering open questions can truly be the key to lowering your anxiety and having engaging discussions with the people you meet.

Yes, extroverts can ask open questions too, but they may very well have already flitted onto the next person, not concerned about how deeply they have connected with the person they just met. While they are off looking for the party, you can be having meaningful conversations.

And people WILL want to talk to you.

When you ask questions that engage others, they will want to share with you.

People love to talk about themselves, so if you present yourself with confidence, have a great greeting and ask open questions of the people you meet, you will find yourself engaged in conversation.

For this reason, mastering open questions can be your SECRET KEY to getting people to talk.

From Closed to Open - Exercise

Rewrite these closed questions as open questions.

For example:

"Do you want to go for lunch today?" – closed question

"Where do you want to go for lunch today?" – open question

"Did you like this morning's speaker?"

"Are you going away for Christmas?"

"Do you play a musical instrument?"

"Are you just visiting?"

"Do you have any ideas to add?"

"Are there any questions?"

"Do you like kayaking?"

"Did you have a good vacation?"

"Do you like to travel?"

"Did you enjoy college?"

"Do you want me to phone you?"

"Do you like sunny days?"

"Do you like to go for long drives?"

"Do you like juice?"

"You've met Sally before, right?"

Possible Responses

How did you make out?

Here are some examples of how these closed questions can be transformed into open questions:

"Did you like this morning's speaker?"

"What did you think of this morning's speaker?"

"How did you like this morning's speaker?"

"What did you like best about this morning's speaker?"

"Are you going away for Christmas?"

"Where are you going for Christmas?"

"What are you doing for Christmas?"

"Do you play a musical instrument?"

"What musical instruments do you play?"

"Are you just visiting?"

"Where are you visiting from?"

"Do you have any ideas to add?"

"What ideas do you have to add?"

"Are there any questions?"

"What questions do you have?"

"What questions are there?"

"Do you like kayaking?"

"What do you like about kayaking?"

"What water sports do you like?"

"Did you have a good vacation?"

"What was the best part about your vacation?"

"Tell me about your vacation."

"Do you like to travel?"

"What types of travel do you like to do?"

"Tell me about your travel experiences."

"Did you enjoy college?"

"What did you enjoy about college?"

"What was college like for you?"

"Do you want me to phone you?"

"How do you want me to follow up with you?"

"Do you like sunny days?"

"What do you like to do on sunny days?"

"Do you like to go for long drives?"

"If you had time today for a long drive, where would you go?"

"Do you like juice?"

"What is your favorite type of juice?"

"You've met Sally before, right?"

"When and how did you meet Sally?"

Leading Questions

Have a look at this next set of questions and see what you notice?

"Do you want to go for lunch today?"

"Do you want to go to Ben's Burger's for lunch?"

"Where do you want to go for lunch today?"

You will probably have recognized the first and second questions as being closed questions, and the last question as being an open question. But what is different about the second question?

Clue: What do you think the questioner wants to hear in response?

The second question is what is referred to as a 'leading' question

"Do you want to go for lunch today?" – closed question

"Do you want to go to Ben's Burger's for lunch?" – leading question

"Where do you want to go for lunch today?" – open question

A leading question is any question in which you 'telegraph' your desired response.

For example:

"You like working at this office, right?"

"We had a great time at the party, didn't we?"

"What are the worst parts of working Saturdays?"

The reason that leading questions are not desirable is that they are not getting at what the other person thinks. They are actually manipulative, though generally without malicious intent. And they aren't going to help you become an accomplished conversationalist.

From Leading to Open - Exercise

Rewrite these leading questions into non-leading open questions.

"Do you have conflicts with your supervisor?"

"How fast was the Mercedes going before it hit the BMW?"

"Don't you hate flying?"

"Well, that was a great seminar, wasn't it?"

"How much time will the new process save you?"

"Did you have a good day at school?"

"How was your awesome vacation?"

"Did you like our new styles?"

"Did you enjoy the team-building activity?"

"You have a great boss, don't you?"

"Wasn't that movie exciting?"

"What parts of the new software are the hardest to adapt to?"

Possible Responses

How did you make out with these questions?

Here are some possibilities of how these leading questions can be transformed into open questions:

"Do you have conflict with your supervisor?"

"What is your relationship like with your supervisor?"

"How fast was the Mercedes going before it hit the BMW?"

"How fast was each car going before they collided?"

"Don't you hate flying?"

"How you do you find flying?"

"Well, that was a great seminar, wasn't it?"

"What did you think of the seminar?"

"How much time will the new process save you?"

"How will the new processes affect your productivity?"

"Did you have a good day at school?"

"What was your day at school like today?"

"How was your awesome vacation?"

"How was your vacation?"

"What was the highlight of your vacation?"

"Did you like our new styles?"

"What was your reaction to our new styles?"

"Did you enjoy the team-building activity?"

"What did you think of the team-building activity?"

"You have a great boss, don't you?"

"What's your boss like?"

"Wasn't that movie exciting?"

"What did you think of that movie?"

"What parts of the new software are the hardest to adapt to?"

"What has your experience been adapting to the new software?"

As we wrap up this chapter, here are a few helpful caveats to keep in mind:

As an introvert, you are naturally a good listener. As you apply yourself to learning active listening skills, you will be beginning to take your natural abilities to a higher level.

Messages are conveyed by the words spoken (10%), tone of voice (40%) and body language (50%).

Use active listening by giving the speaker your full attention.

Ask more open questions than closed questions.

Avoid leading questions that 'telegraph' the desired answer.

Non-verbal communication carries a powerful message (more on this next in Chapter 6).

Voice tone also matters (more on this in Chapter 11).

What do you think? After learning about the fundamentals, what do you think your strengths are? Where are your biggest opportunities for improvement?

Case Studies

Rebecca found the techniques of clarifying and summarizing to be most helpful. Not only did she find she understood more when she took time to clarify, but summarizing conversations led to her being asked to summarize meetings, which allowed her to structure opportunities for her own input to be heard.

Larry found the active listening to be a particularly helpful skill, not only at work but at home as well. Forcing himself to put down his phone, and stop thinking ahead immediately resulted in more revealing conversations and deeper connections with loved ones.

Chris was delighted to learn that she could substitute open questions for closed questions and keep the other person talking longer!

Kelly was astounded at how many leading questions he used to ask. When he stopped using them, he noticed people shared a lot more with him.

The Introvert's Survival Guide to Active Listening

Active listening is the key to people feeling heard and to you getting the full story from a person.

Here are a few do's and don'ts to keep in mind:

Do's

DO listen to what the other person is saying.

DO pay attention to their words, their tone of voice and their body language.

DO give cues that you are listening (eye contact, nodding).

DO ask clarifying questions.

DO summarize to check understanding.

Don'ts

DON'T think about your response while the other person is speaking.

DON'T interrupt the person you are listening to.

DON'T have an agenda.

3 Keys to Remember

KEY 1: Use active listening.

KEY 2: Don't think about your response.

KEY 3: Pay attention to the whole message.

The Introvert's Survival Guide to Asking Questions

Your ability to ask thoughtful open questions is your best tool for getting people to open up to you.

Here are a few do's and don'ts to keep in mind:

Do's

DO ask open questions.

DO think ahead about the questions you will ask.

DO ask follow-up questions.

DO use active listening.

DO take a few notes, if needed.

Don'ts

DON'T ask closed questions.

DON'T 'telegraph' the answer you are seeking by asking leading questions.

3 Keys to Remember

KEY 1: Use open questions and avoid closed or leading questions.

KEY 2: Listen actively to the answers.

KEY 3: If in doubt, ask another question.

# Chapter 19:  Expanding The Limits

Did you ever wonder why you tap your feet whenever you listen to a good music, or why you become teary-eyed when a certain part of a song moves your heart? It's amazing how something intangible can penetrate your soul. During moments you feel misunderstood, there's always music to let you know that in some place in this earth, someone understands.

When you listen to your favorite song, it makes no sense to say that the drums sound better than the guitar. Or the piano sounds better than the bass. Each instrument contributes to the beauty of the song.

The way how the notes impeccably blend with each other makes the song more than a song. It establishes a connection between you and the people behind the song that speech cannot even fathom. This is maybe because of what all of you encompass in common: a fascination towards the inner-world. You share something that cannot be seen by the naked eye and only your soul understands. As Mitch Albom perfectly puts it, "Everyone joins a band in this life. And what you play affects someone. Sometimes, it affects the world."

UPSIDES OF INTROVERSION

For a long time, people have been living in a hyper-outgoing culture. As people get more and more engaged with this extroversion hype, the more they get tired of chasing the fulfillment of life. This has set the world to explore and embrace the mysteries that introspection holds. People are convinced of the balance it can bring to the society. As they chose to embrace introversion, they gradually recognized the benefits it can give.

The Benefit of Solitude

Life is full of stress. Majority of your week are spent with work or school. The endless to-do list robs you of sleep, relaxation and opportunities to have fun. However, if you strongly agree that life is not merely about a series of finished tasks, then you must pay attention to the value of silence and solitude.

Solitude is a practice of being momentarily absent from the midst of other people and things so you can be alone with your thoughts and emotions. It breaks your "have-to-do-this" mindset by slowing your body down. Instead of burning a bunch of cash on therapy, just sit down in a quiet place and you'll experience the serenity your soul is longing for. By simply embracing your introversion, you are walking towards a life balanced by solitude.

Solitude disconnects you from the world for a while and bonds you deeply in your soul. By helping you create inner space, solitude clears the clouds in your mind so you can make wise decisions and unleash your creativity. According to research, most introverts have a habit of carefully thinking things through before acting. As you rest your soul in its tranquility, you'll become more self-aware, refreshed and self-disciplined. You'll have more value towards thoughtfulness, moral integrity and empathy for almost everyone around you.

The Benefit of Discipline

Discipline is your way of making your choices, decisions and actions. If you ask successful people about their secret in achieving their goals, the answer would be proper discipline. You can dream high. You can envision a lot of possibilities, but if you ignore the value of discipline, you will not get anywhere fast.

Discipline cultivates a strong determination in you that will inspire you to do the things that you want. It gives you the nerve and confidence to face challenges and obstacles which form you in becoming a better individual.

Accomplishing things is much easier with time management. Discipline also yields a positive outlook in life. Staying well-ordered helps you work well thus keeps you away from draining tension. Live a life full of self-confidence and enthusiasm by being properly disciplined.

However, developing discipline requires plenty of inward reflections. To maintain your focus better, you need to converse constantly with yourself. There will always be distractions that will block your way and point you in a different direction. You have to keep reminding yourself which way you should go. Stepping inside the world of introversion takes you one step closer to a disciplined life.

The Benefit of Creativity

Creativity is the ability to form new things or ideas. Imagination is what fired the world's development. Creativity is the reason for all of the modern conveniences you enjoy today and why many more are still coming.

Creativity is not just about arts and crafts. In one article in Psychology Today, Carlin Flora writes, "Buying into a limited definition of creativity prevents many from appreciating their own potential."

As you explore website blogs and YouTube blogs, you'll find many people posting DIY (Do It Yourself) tutorials about home décor, equipment, clothing tips, etc. It shows how much you can be creative about everything under the sun.

Being creative also gives a lot more payoffs. It generates balance and order in life by providing a sense of control over external things. As a result, it gives you a more positive atmosphere. It gives you a greater sense of comfort and personal growth.

Have you seen a child quietly enjoying his new set of crayons and coloring books? At first, you'll find it funny why a cat suddenly becomes violet, or a girl has green hair. However, as you watch how he was having fun coloring those images, you can sense the fulfillment on his face. This is because creativity enhances the spiritual and mental aspects of life. It makes thoughts and feelings clearer. And creativity can only be rooted from a healthy inner life.

Since longing for solitude is a natural habit for introverts, it gives them more room for creativity. Laurie Helgoe, author of Introvert Power, said that, "There's a lot of evidence that boredom is a precursor to creativity, and introverts are more welcoming of the solitude that engenders boredom."

The Benefit of Strong Relationships

As mentioned earlier in this book, introverts are not anti-social. They just focus more on internal foundations of friendships that actually limits their friendliness.

Life is hard to imagine without the people you love around you. Without relationships, life makes no sense at all. Why do you have to pursue your dreams? Why would you even need to become better if it wasn't for the people you love?

By learning how to share internal things, like your random thoughts, emotional struggles and confusions, you can create stronger relationships. By establishing strong relationships, you allow yourself to experience the real essence of being connected with other people.

# Chapter 20: Learning To Socialize As An Introvert

The surprising fact about learning is that it is a "never end" journey. Learning is continuous. One starts to learn right from childhood to adulthood. Even as an elderly person, one still continues with the journey of learning. Being an introvert does not spare one of the process. You have to learn to improve yourself as a person. And to improve yourself, you have to learn the art of socializing. Since it will not be any way easy, you just have to take the step one after the other by learning from others just like every child.

Let us take a child as an example. A child learns gradually but continuously. At first, he or she learns to crawl. After months of crawling, a child learns to stand through his or her mother. After that, he or she begins to walk, taking one step at a time, gently. Later, he or she studies how people walk and then starts to walk like them, faster. He or she soon learns how to talk. Thus, every learning process that a child passes through is through others around him or her. His or her growth still goes on endlessly, for learning is a sea that has no end.

As an introvert, why don't you adopt the learning techniques of a child? For a child does not learn everything at a time, he or she learns at a snail's pace. As an introvert, why don't you hide some of those traits for some time and start to learn through others? Of course you can. Like a child, all you have to do is to take the following steps one after the other.

Force yourself to do that Thing you would not want to do

Contemplating on whether to be the first to stretch a hand of greeting to your business colleague or not? Thinking whether to invite a "not so close" friend of yours over to your house to spend some minutes with you? Go ahead! It may seem very difficult at first, but try to force yourself that once, and you will find it a bit easier next time. Walk up to that your business colleague and open your arms of greeting. Invite that distant friend to your own house for a lunch. You are going to find those gestures helpful. The business colleague who has been avoiding you before will be the first to greet you the following day. That distant friend, having enjoyed your lunch, will also be forced to reciprocate the gesture. This way, the bond becomes stronger in no time. Remember the secret? Just force yourself. Got it? Yeah! Now let us move on.

Meet New People Every Day

Even if getting to meet new people per day will want to appear too tiring, try to meet at least one person in a day. By meeting new people at the turns of days, you would have added so many names to the list of the people you have known, say, at the end of a month. A person whom you have invited for a meal will be glad to introduce you to his or her other friends.

Thus, you meet new faces, although you may not necessarily need to form a serious relationship with them.

Try to Lend a Helping Hand to People

Although you may not have the capability to help people all the time; when you don't have, let people around you know that you are concerned. If you have, let your neighbors know that you have. Let people around your house see you as a philanthropist if you are the type that is wealthy. That way, you will be endeared to them. Should there be any program organized by any of your neighbors, such a neighbor will be encouraged to invite you. And through invitation, you will mix up with others, getting more attached to people and getting more involved in social programs. An introvert who always shows readiness in lending people a hand of help will be forced into relating with them even without him or her knowing.

Visit your Family Members at your Leisure Time

Do not spend the whole of your free time alone. Visit members of your family occasionally, and interact with them. If you are the fellow that comes from an extended family, relate more with other members of your family. Do not restrict your relationship to your parents and siblings alone. Move the relationship beyond your parents' house. Visit beautiful places with them. Ask them to take you to places that they think you need to know. For instance, tell a distant family member to take you out, not your immediate family member. He or she will be happy to go out with you, especially if he or she knows you as an introvert. That way, you will learn to socialize as an introvert.

# Chapter 21: The Useless Envy

Extravert Envy. If it sounds familiar, you are most likely an introvert. It exists but rarely talked about. Mostly because the taciturns are embarrassed to admit it while the expressives are probably too busy being exuberant to notice.

I Sociable and People-person

Extraverts. They have an air about them that makes people comfortable to be around him. They are sociable with people they know and the strangers they just met. It's like having a direct line to what makes people tick. The things they can do with that ability and knowledge. It's being relaxed in a public setting that is most enviable. They are so relaxed that it doesn't matter if they are suddenly picked out from the group to answer a question, they can easily answer with wit and humor. It seems like nothing can faze them.

Introverts. Imagine having the big weight of sociability lifted off of your shoulders. You can probably just walk to a stranger and start a very engaging conversation with her. You'll find out you have similar hobbies (at least one) then other people would notice and they can join in. Later on, you can exchange emails so the two of you can continue chatting. The weekend is near so maybe you can meet up again and chat some more in person.

Off the top of your head, did that immediately feel like a liberating feeling?

Does it feel more like a chore? An energy draining chore?

Imagine doing that tomorrow. And the next day. And the next day.

Can you stomach it?

If you answer, "No. Yes. No" then you are a true introvert. If you answered otherwise, then you are either an extravert or the almost mythical creature that rests in the middle of the spectrum and can fluctuate from one personality to another. The word, "people" is an introvert's weakness. It cannot be easily passed around without at least invoking a sense of dread. So why would a perfectly good taciturn want to be a crucible for her weakness? It does not make sense. In exchange for being sociable, the joy of solitude that recharges you will disappear. Those new found friends will be calling and asking you things that you do not really want to answer. Introverts likes to listen and sadly this downgrade approach to what has been initially set can disappoint the new friend. She thought you are as bright and cheerful as her. Then the regret and disappointment envelopes you. It always seems to happen. Trying to be an extravert for a few days is more than possible—it is one of the many introverts advantage, but staying that way is exhausting. These new friends either understand your introversion or they are going to have to find new ones.

II Happy and Fast

Extraverts. It almost seems that extraverts have a bottomless pit filled with positive emotions. They are cheerful, energetic, and enthusiastic about almost everything new or old. The always happy people. People from the other end of the spectrum would often wonder where they get their energy from. The expressives are very difficult to catch up to especially that they have this "dive-in first, think later" attitude. Work load can go by them easily because they like to process everything in a faster pace and they love to work in groups. This is why they are favored in the working environment—everyone gets along with them, they get the work done right and fast.

Introverts. To work at a speed that can impress the bosses? Most introverts will sign up in a heartbeat. There would be no need to spend hours just figuring out how to compose a single report in a way that is appealing to all. It would just be done. But then again, that means you will no longer have that precious time to really think and understand what you are doing. What if you wrote down something wrong? Worse, what if somebody asks you about it and you couldn't answer because you were only focusing on completing it fast? It will be so embarrassing and that is one of the things that terrifies you.

The power of introverts lies in their ability to understand everything before acting on it. They are able to proudly reiterate what they have done, explain how they've come to it and make very informed decisions with very little risks. Aren't those worthy of the boss' praises? Not only do you comply with what is required of you and also able to get the joy of re-discovering yourself in the process—something that extroverts will never understand because they are too busy jumping from one work load to another. If you think about it, this may just be their defense mechanism so they do not have to go through a possibly devastating reflection. No introvert will give up working alone and working undisturbed. It is a source of serenity and contentment in a workplace that is full of noise.

Who ever said that happiness is only achieved by specific positive emotions such as exuberance, cheerfulness and enthusiasm? It is a dogma set by society who loves the expressives. Happiness to the taciturns is the feeling of serenity, steadiness, stability, contentment, calmness and deep love. These are the things that last longer and the taciturns feel this way every time they are in solitude. If you are happy with what you've always done, why do you need to be someone different?

III Spontaneous and Grounded

Extraverts. It seems that caution is not strong in them which is good because they have only a few scruples to hold them back from experiencing the wonders of life. Obviously, they are explorers and adventurers constantly looking for excitement on a daily basis. They meet everyday obstacles with open arms and an optimistic world view. It makes sense because they always like to tell stories that can amaze people. Do you remember the direct line they have on people? It seems that they also receive news through that because extraverts are always up to date about the on-goings of a certain environment. They keep their feet firmly planted on reality. They rarely fantasize or daydream and often wonder how other people can find the time to do that when the world is already a dream waiting to be explored.

Introverts. A taciturn must look quite sad for an extravert who does not understand why you are not like them. They must wonder how you can stay in one place and not be bothered by the on-goings around you. Why not have a little adventure? The extravert is right. You are not bothered. Because while he is moving from place to place to find excitement, you stay in one place studying something in a subjective level. You look at it thoroughly and form your opinion about it. That is exciting for you. While the expressives take the trains, planes or buses to have their adventures, yours is already happening. You direct the experience within. Ride a horse and use a bow and arrow? You did that in less than one hour and you didn't even budge. It isn't like you are never going out. You will. The vacation just needs to be well thought of, planned and prepared for. You do not want to take unnecessary risks. The feeling of self-preservation is second nature to you and without it, you would not know how to protect yourself. Everyone has their own adventures—it's just a matter of how a person goes through with it that's different.

One of an introvert's favorite abilities is to listen. Yes, it involves people, possibly the expressives, talking about their day and everything else. It is not boring. You never thought of it that way. Listening is another way you explore. Perhaps not the physical world but the inner world of a person. There is that surge of enjoyment when you've realized something about them that they were too busy to notice. How can you ever think about giving up this unique perception into people? However exciting looking an extrovert's approach is when it comes to people, work, and life, it will never be as satisfying as they think it is for introverts.

# Conclusion

Thank you again for downloading this book!

I hope this book was able to help you to clear some dilemmas and questions you probably had about introverted people whether you are yourself an introvert or someone close to you is.

If this book has helped in any way to feel better, to start working on your self-esteem or to understand a bit more yourself, your introverted friends, children or partner, then this book met my goal and I'm very pleased about that. And finally to get back to basics and remind you that before you can change yourself you have to accept yourself completely as you are.

Thank you and good luck!

www.ingramcontent.com/pod-product-compliance
Lightning Source LLC
Chambersburg PA
CBHW060324030426
42336CB00011B/1193